the
natural eclectic

written and photographed by

heather ross

the natural eclectic

a design aesthetic inspired by nature

Figure.1
Vancouver / Berkeley

contents

{ SUZANNE DIMMA }

foreword

THE NATURAL ECLECTIC is a visual homage to the power of simple organic beauty in the world around us.

This thoughtfully curated book is for anyone with an appreciation for the art of assemblage, styling and decorating, who is driven by an appreciation for nature and who loves to be surrounded with the things that move them most.

A photographer, stylist, writer, shop owner, painter and now author, Heather Ross is a true Renaissance woman. Her infectious personality and unbridled enthusiasm for all things natural is apparent in everything she does.

Having worked with Heather for many years, I have always admired her ability as a photographer to capture the emotion behind the image. Whether it is relaxed beach shacks on Savary Island or a modern glass masterpiece on the rugged shoreline of West Vancouver, she always catches that elusive moment of magic that all magazine editors hope for. She has a unique talent for creating beautifully lit, beautifully imagined storytelling through pictures.

Heather's eye for spotting the inspirational in the everyday never fails to impress. She is a tireless treasure hunter—seeking out, editing and assembling wonderfully patinated finds from the sea, the woods, yard sales and flea markets. She can take a collection of ephemera and create a compelling vignette that speaks to us on a soulful level. In essence, she brings a human quality to the found object.

From her, we can learn to conjure grace and art where none exists. To change a small corner of our lives just by transforming a few unique finds into a pleasing still life.

I can only imagine the world seen through Heather's eyes, where inspiration is everywhere and the possibilities are endless. Happily, there's now a book that helps us do just that.

the natural eclectic
philosophy

THE FIRST DAY I put pen to paper and started writing this book, I made a discovery. I had set out into a very damp afternoon feeling slightly bogged down by the unusually cold spring, when a bright little bit of something caught my attention from the grass at the sidewalk's edge. To my delight, it was a robin's eggshell! In that moment, all the glee of childhood rushed back. I cupped that tiny treasure in my hand and took in its magic.

I spotted a teeny hole where a small beak had chipped away, breaking free into a new world. All my favorite colors: bluey green mottled with tones of beige and grey, offset by the creamy-white frayed and brittle edges in the smooth exterior. Fragile yet strong, pure and simple in form, the speckles so random and organic, the colors serene and gentle. Elegant and perfect in its imperfections—a find! And what an auspicious way to begin a new project.

This is what *The Natural Eclectic* is all about—a philosophy as opposed to a style. With this book, I invite you to delve beneath the surface and explore a lifestyle that not only is nuanced with grace and beauty, but also is deeply personal, multilayered and connected to the natural world. The naturally eclectic home is filled with belongings imbued with meaning and memories, honest materials of a certain integrity and timelessness—a home that evolves and transitions with the seasons.

I believe that nurturing an appreciation for nature—an awareness of the cycles of life, the seasons and all creatures great and small—improves not just our sense of well-being but also our global environment. Actually *experiencing* the elements is so powerful and moving. Observing how the moon rises and falls, listening to the soft rustle as we walk amongst grasses, feeling the pull of the tide . . . these moments remind us that we are connected to the natural world. There is something very magical and grounding in this.

Throughout *The Natural Eclectic*, I encourage you to get out and experience nature, to forage and to use your imagination when creating a home. It's amazing what natural treasures can be found even within an urban environment. Just go down a lane and you'll come across decorative weeds, grasses, falling leaves—and maybe even a robin's egg! Look to nature in all its grand and humble beauty; look within to find your own creative voice.

As a "natural eclectic," I am drawn to so many materials and themes in design and the natural world. I don't want to limit my expression to just one medium—I want to convey all that inspires me in everything I do. My approach lies in the multilayered meanings of these words "natural" and "eclectic."

I draw inspiration from the duality of the word *natural*. Most often, it conveys that which is derived from or inspired by nature and organic materials. Yet I find particular resonance in an alternate meaning of *natural*: that which is genuine, innate, sincere, spontaneous and uncontrived. I think of natural as something that unfolds with ease. Just as nature seems to effortlessly present raw beauty and harmony, when we approach something naturally, we impart so much more grace than when we contrive something.

In the world of design, the word *eclectic* is commonly used to mean mixing one period style with another. I use the word in a more all-encompassing sense. I choose individual items for their unique charm *regardless* of their lineage or source. Derived from "pick out," *eclectic* as I use the word means to seek out and gather the best elements of all global philosophies, styles, ideas.

I grew up on the West Coast of Canada and I have also lived in Paris. I've beachcombed along many shores and searched for alluring treasures in antique markets across Europe. My aesthetic has been informed by both natural and cultural adventures.

I've always loved treasure hunting and putting things together, but I never called it decorating. I love gathering and foraging, but I never considered it flower arranging. Labels and trends go out of style, but authentic philosophies, values and interests reside on a deeper, more lasting level. I've explored ceramics, textile design, printmaking, painting, photography, styling and writing. At times I've been called an artist, other times a designer or a craftsperson. I just like to think of myself as a person who enjoys creating in many forms. This is actually one of the reasons I opened up a shop—so I could bring together my many loves and showcase them where like-minded people might enjoy them. Since I opened my Vancouver boutique in 2001, countless individuals have responded to my evocative look and the way I mix things up.

People often remark on my signature color palette that is inspired by the coast. They're also drawn to the way I incorporate natural materials and found objects into my curated displays and vignettes. More importantly, they share how tranquil my space makes them feel. Yet they often seem at a loss as to how to create this themselves. Within these pages I share insights into my own process.

Some of us have an innate talent, eye or sense of things, just as a musical person has an ear for tone. I also believe you can cultivate an ability to be more attuned to your environment, and enrich your life by your efforts. Listen to yourself and your senses, pay attention to what moves you, collect and cherish the things that inspire you. Do you prefer to be in a soft meadow or looking out upon a great expanse of sea? Do you prefer the sheen of silk or the rough, hand-hewn texture of linen? Begin by connecting in a sensory way to all you do—seeing, feeling, touching.

While I'm a highly visual person, I also love to express myself through the written word. It just seemed a natural fit to one day have a book filled with all my thoughts and images. Whereas most "creatives" focus on one role, I love to have my hand in many things, to see a whole concept evolve. I immersed myself deeply in the creation of this book, not just with words and images but also all the juxtapositions and nuances, to create a singularity of vision that I feel is an extension of myself. The creation of this book is a lifelong dream come true. From the time I was very young, I wanted not just to make things, but to share the things I made. As an adult, I came to learn that this was my way of feeling connected. This sharing evokes a feeling in others and in turn elevates my own purpose and joy, and gives me a sense of belonging in the world.

Reading this book, you may realize, "I'm a natural eclectic too." How it manifests in your life may be different, yet we can still be kindred spirits sharing the same values and inspirations. Nature has been the greatest teacher in my life, and creativity the greatest gift. In nature, I feel at peace. When I am finding beauty and capturing it, I feel I am doing exactly what I'm meant to do. Immersed in the moment, I feel true joy in knowing that this is my place in life. My authentic self. We all have our own authentic voice . . . and this is mine.

beauty, elegance and eclecticism

HAVE BEEN DRAWN to beauty my whole life. As an artist and photographer, I cannot help but be captivated by the depths of our world's beauty, even amidst the chaos. Yet, at times I've also wrestled with the notion of beauty. With so much struggle in our lives, is it superficial to behold and uphold the beautiful?

I believe that, even (or especially) in the midst of hardship, small pauses to observe beauty bring us peace and uplift us. Across all cultures, people are universally inspired by the unfolding of a blossom and the dazzling array of colors at sundown. Those of us who are especially attuned to beauty are not naive to the sufferings of the world; quite the contrary. The gift of heightened senses and the ability to find splendor in the smallest of things also mean vulnerability. To truly embrace the subtle nuances of life, we must be open and receptive.

While attending art school, I had an experience that would shape my creative path for years. At the age of nineteen I received a scholarship for my artistic achievement, and I was excited to be accepted into the second year of an acclaimed art school. I flourished in printmaking and ceramics; instructors and students alike remarked on a certain Zen harmony to my work. Yet in my painting class, this same aesthetically pleasing quality was trivialized and frowned upon.

Studying alongside me in my year was a particularly talented and provocative group of painters who exploded onto the international art scene with their highly charged works. With my subtle, evocative paintings, I felt invisible beside them, or at times even mocked for my inherent sense of beauty. For the first time in my life, the very quality that came naturally to me was being challenged. All of a sudden, I found myself in a realm where beauty worked against me.

This was a confusing time, and I felt alienated. Beauty had become a bad word. So I left art school and shifted my energies, channeling my strengths into the design world. I worked with my hands as an artisan, enjoying the tactile materiality of things, free from the rhetoric of the art world.

Twenty years would pass before I would meet a brilliant artist, Brent, who reassured me that there was a place for beauty in art. He felt I belonged to the beauty of the world. Encouraged by his insights, I found my voice as an artist and started painting again. The moment I let go of my concerns about other people's perceptions and embraced myself as an artist who naturally responds to beauty, a whole new series of work unfolded.

I believe that for something to resonate as beautiful, it has to be authentic; otherwise, it comes off as artifice. Looking back, I am surprised I let my creative spirit be crushed by this one experience in art school. Perhaps as a young, impressionable *female* student, I was particularly sensitive to being critiqued for the harmony in my work, when I was in no way striving to just create works that were "decorative" or "pretty." True beauty is deep and moving and strikes us intellectually and emotionally as well as visually.

So how does this translate into my current philosophy of lifestyle and design? The value of an eclectic philosophy is its embrace of light and dark, yin and yang, new and old. Eclecticism allows for both the masculine and the feminine.

HEATHER ROSS
Misty pale azura sea
36 x 36 in
Acrylic on canvas

This arrangement feels ethereal yet also rustic and organic. The unfolding fluted forms impart a delicateness to the surface of this weighty handmade vessel, while eucalyptus leaves create a feathery display of shadow and light.

Simply including a fine white coral branch or lacy remnant of lichen can bring a lighter touch to a rustic or moody tableau.

Sometimes in an effort to be pretty, the excess of decorative qualities, or the feminine, can actually have an *inverse* effect. You can easily pretty up a room; just paint a new wall color, bring in some fluffy pillows, stack some cupcakes on a tower of milk glass, and you're ready to go. But you can transform a space into something more alluring and unique with the inclusion of a few unpredictable grounding aspects and some thoughtful, more personal touches. Let some light in, yet balance it with earthy elements.

At the other end of the spectrum is the current trend toward very raw and moody table-scapes with styling approaches so dark they emulate the muted tones of the Dutch Masters. While these tableaux have a certain rich appeal, they can border on bleak or austere if executed with a heavy hand. The same could be said of the industrial/factory trend. I love patina and worn, decayed surfaces, and I believe that old, battered items can look fabulous in an old brick loft or as a counterpoint to an expansive contemporary home of concrete and glass.

Most newer apartments and small homes, though, would drown in the scale and gravity of rough, masculine furnishings fashioned out of scrappy wood, metal and leather. Over time, as trends shift, one might regret investing in large, bulky industrial-style items, especially

We can take cues from nature. Note the poetic juxtaposition of delicate pink cherry blossoms scattered upon an earthy lichen-encrusted stump.

ROYAL YEAST
Make Perfect Bread

STRIKE THE RIGHT BALANCE
Mix funky old industrial items with lighter, more graceful forms.

if the purchases are reproductions instead of the real deal.

I am not cautioning against any one trend or effect so much as warning against the pitfall of fashioning a look with a single note. This can become stale and dated over time, and is especially inflexible if executed in a formulaic manner that leaves out your own personality.

So, while it's only human to be influenced by lifestyle trends, consider a mingled look that does not slant all the way in one direction or another. Create a home that can transition and evolve over time (just as you do) without costly mistakes and drastic changes. Add to, subtract from and curate your home as you are influenced by world movements. We are not beholden to live just one way within a certain decade or style. We can cherish and acquire things that speak to us for their innate charm and present them artfully within our surroundings as our lives evolve.

My personal aesthetic has been consistent my whole life, yet within it there is great variety. I am inspired by organic forms, and yet I have a classical, rather graphic and linear sense of composition. While most of my home is light and airy, I have a feature wall in dark charcoal grey that provides a weighty backdrop to an assemblage of ethereal art and bleached ocean treasures.

While I love rusty old patinas, matte clay vessels, barnacled surfaces and coarse weaves, I think they're enhanced by notes of elegance

and sophistication. Many of the furnishings in my home are distressed, with layers of worn-down paint, yet I also like glossy white surfaces that allow the fabulous patinas of other objects to stand out. You can inject an elevated sense of beauty into an otherwise earthy or edgy space with just a few delicate touches in the form of lustrous objects.

NEITHER EXPENSE nor pedigree is necessary to achieve an elegant room. All you need is a deft eye and an essential awareness of understated beauty. Indeed, this involves a certain polish and refinement, but it can come in the humblest of forms. The Japanese have a term, *wabi-sabi*, which is similar to this quintessential quality. It refers to a rustic aesthetic that embraces the innately beautiful flaws in primitive-yet-poetic forms.

An atmosphere or attitude of perfection is not alluring. Perfection can be intimidating, unwelcoming and altogether impractical.

Striving for perfection is pointless, for we will never achieve it. Because of my aesthetic sensibility, people often imagine that my home is perfect. Let me be clear—I am not an interior designer, and I do not live in a mansion in the countryside. You will see corners and cameos of my personal space throughout this book—areas that especially delight me. But my home is not a showpiece. I have a simple garden-level corner suite in the city, with French doors that open out to a beautiful patio garden. I can walk to my beloved boutique, just five blocks east, or down to the seashore, six blocks north. It is where I share my time with the ones I love, putter in the garden, tinker and curate vignettes with the natural treasures I find. Guests to my home may be quite surprised (but pleasantly so) to discover that it might be a little messy at times. My home is small, and because I love things and have my hands in many projects day and night, it can get tousled!

WABI-SABI

The Japanese use this term to refer to a rustic aesthetic that embraces the innately beautiful flaws of primitive yet poetic forms.

Throughout this book, you'll see corners and cameos of my space— but it's not a showpiece. It's where I share time with loved ones, enjoy tea in the garden, tinker and create.

Being a self-employed artist, I have learned how to create an enjoyable life on rather humble means, taking pleasure in simple things like having tea in my garden.

So let's not confuse quality of life with riches or opulence. Elegance is neither excessive, wasteful, boastful nor loud. There is a certain understated grace in the presence of an elegant person or environment. It is seductive in its simplicity, and carefully distilled. For me, the key to elegance is subtlety. When something is elegant, you just know it, yet it's hard to define what makes it so.

My desire for elegant beauty comes from a place of seeking serenity, along with a desire to be engaged, inspired, captivated. I encourage you to define and seek out that which *feels* beautiful to you and to manifest this beauty in your life.

elemental living

OFTEN DESCRIBE both my paintings and the atmospheres I create as "elemental." Am I referring to the elements of earth, water, air and fire? Or am I using *elemental* to describe what is fundamental, pared down to its purest essence? Or to the actual elements, such as pure metals, of which our material world is made?

I am speaking to all of the above. To embrace the elemental in a personal living space means to ground the home in raw, natural materials, connect it to the landscape and the ever-changing seasons and elements, and provide all the essential comforts of living without need for lavish ornamentation. I distinguish elemental artworks and interiors by their elegant use of space and materials. A simple bowl could be described as elemental because of the choice of material but also because of its restrained design.

Out of necessity, we live in shelters to protect ourselves from the elemental forces of nature, yet this can disconnect us from our environment. Great architecture takes the elements into consideration, factoring in how a home is situated within a landscape, helping to join us and our sheltering structures with the natural world. Fortunately, the use of glass allows us to see our sky as it changes in all its gentle hues from morning until nightfall.

Let's explore the elements.

The striking use of glass, stone and concrete in this waterfront home designed by Zacharko Yustin Architects seamlessly connects the structure to the elements of earth, water and air.

The element of air is most often invisible to us—until we see it shape-shifting in the wonderful drama of weather. Fresh air is essential to healthy living. Allowing it in through open windows and French doors is a wonderful way to breathe life into a home. Having both outdoor and indoor spaces allows us to seek sunshine or shade in sheltered patio and garden settings as the elemental forces of nature change. At times we each need a breath of fresh air to clear our head and help us find a refreshing new way of seeing things.

In my chapter on color, I explore my preference for a slightly cooler palette, as I find it so serene. That said, I do not like *being* cold. I love warmth, and one of my favorite things to do is to sit by a roaring fire in my home. Candles, ambient lighting and a warm, crackling hearth bring the comforting element of fire into a space. A campfire or pit fire outdoors is another magical way to draw people around a fire and enjoy its primordial power. When humankind discovered how to make fire, we began to transform natural materials in magical ways. Metals could be melted and earth could be baked and transformed by something other than just the sun. These simple methods and resources still provide for our modern lives.

Our homes are built on, and often made of, earth. Terra-cotta, used for making bricks and tiles, literally means cooked earth. The earth's crust gives us sand, silica, flint, agate and beautiful crystals such as rose quartz and amethyst. When mixed with organic plant and animal material, rocks and minerals break down into clay. Have you ever considered, while lifting a fine porcelain teacup to your lips, that it was artfully crafted from the simple material of mud? In the seventh and eighth centuries, the Chinese were the first to use a white kaolin clay to make what we've come to call "china."

I grew up near a beach that had clay in pockets of the tidal pools. As a toddler I would sink my hands into this squishy sediment and form crude mud pies. Years later I enjoyed forming wet clay round and round on a potter's wheel, feeling its rough-yet-slippery texture course through my fingers. So satisfying and sensual. Once the clay pot was dried and fired in a kiln, I would dip it in a glaze (more earth, water and mineral combined) and fire it again, the kiln so hot the silica in the glaze would melt to glass and create its final silky casing on the pot. Perhaps it is these experiences that have connected me so closely to the element of earth.

I consider water to be the most *essential* of the elements. No thing can live without water. No garden, no creature, no person and no home. Water is source; morning tea and cleaning rituals. We are drawn to fire, but water is a fundamental need. Water moves and flows, rises and falls, washes away, washes clean. It revitalizes, brings things to life. Much like our emotions, water is fluid, and it pulls with the moon. It has inspired many a poet and painter, including myself. From crystal-clear to the deepest cerulean blue, it is mercurial in nature. Over time, the sea and its crashing waves and infinite pull grind the rocks, stones and skeletal forms of sea creatures into sand. Sand when struck by fire becomes molten glass, from which we can shape many things. Imagine the fascination when the first person witnessed lightning striking sand, turning it into a glassy liquid! Perhaps this is why when I gaze upon old glass, I feel enchanted, as if I am looking upon the sea in all its myriad moods and tones.

From crystal clear to cerulean blue, water is mercurial in nature. Over time, the sea and its infinite pull grinds stones and skeletal forms into sand. Sand when struck by fire becomes glass. Perhaps this is why I can gaze upon old glass as if I am looking upon the sea.

T
U
B

Raw elemental materials have been constantly adapted throughout history. Precious metals such as gold, silver and copper have been hammered, woven and cast into sculptures, jewelry, fine garments, utensils and, of course, currencies. These source ingredients are still fundamental for design and construction.

Metals form foundations, bind timbers together, deliver water and electricity and adorn our homes.

Look around your home and touch the elements within it. Stone, concrete and marble provide our pillars, our arches, our foundations and the durable floors we walk upon each day.

While I've never been a
minimalist, I am drawn
to simple compositions
and elemental materials,
so at times I've struck a
sparer note in my shop.
The painting seen here,
Falling/Unfolding, was
part of a series I created,
inspired by the surface
of the moon and organic
patterns found on our
own earth's crust.

21

Earth-derived materials react when exposed to air and sunlight. I love wandering down old streets in Europe, surrounded by architecture that has aged exquisitely over time. Faded, peeling, tinted with moss, these eroded surfaces are like works of art to me.

Of course, in modern times we have some interesting design materials such as acrylic, fiberglass and Lucite, but it is the earth-derived materials that excite me most. One of my favorite things about raw, natural materials as opposed to inert synthetics is the subtle patinas they can form over time. Think of the lovely chalky residue that builds on terra-cotta pots in the garden from the minerals and moisture leaching from the soil. As natural objects are exposed to salty sea air, sunlight and moisture, they react. Metals oxidize and tarnish. Porous stone, cement and clay can be etched and sculpted by water. Wood can fade and weather in the elements or become glossy and burnished from human touch. I love wandering down old streets in Europe, surrounded by all the amazing architecture that has aged and degraded so exquisitely over time. Faded, peeling, flaking, tinted with moss, these uniquely eroded and worn surfaces are all like works of art to me.

Most natural materials found in art and everyday objects comprise just a few simple

Inspired by scenes such as this fresco in Todos Santos, Mexico, it occurred to me that "art" is literally in the heart of "earth"!

elemental compounds. Even color is derived from the elements. Bright whites come from zinc, while iron imparts the red or ochre tones associated with rustic earthy pottery and scenic frescoes. Lapis lazuli used to be ground down by hand to create the rich ultramarine blues adorning Egyptian artifacts and Renaissance paintings.

While visual artists have concepts, inspirations and metaphors in their minds, they must have a medium in which to express them. For artisans, the material itself is part of the story. One day while pondering the word *earth*, it occurred to me that "art" is literally in the heart of earth!

While wood, plant materials and animal fiber are made of more than one element and are organic in nature (meaning they have a cycle of life), I consider them elemental in the sense of being fundamental materials used in textiles, crafts and manufacturing. Bowls and beams and baskets were once roots and branches grasping for the sustenance found in the earth. They can be wonderfully shaped, carved, knotted, twisted and woven by the human hand into the finest of objects and furnishings. Throughout the ages, cultures have been harvesting reeds, fibers, roots and bark to weave vessels, baskets and rugs. Some of these utilitarian items are highly collectible today.

I invite you to connect to the source of the materials around you. Choose your materials wisely. Relate to them on a primary level, touch them and allow them to ground you in your daily life. Consider how we've mined and gathered them from our earth and how they have brought us great quality of life, pleasure and purpose.

3

evocative
color

As an artist I know that color is a language all its own—a language that can express and evoke great feeling. While my abstract paintings are most often informed by landscape and weather, my intent is to capture a *mood* rather than depict a scene. I find things that are literal and obvious can lose their draw over time, whereas subtle mystery and layers of tone can engage us eternally. We can look out to the sea and never feel bored; still and serene or churning and turbulent, its depths evoke so much.

An atmosphere can enhance our state of mind, calm us or stimulate us. Just as writers, musicians and filmmakers evoke thoughts and feelings with their art or storytelling, we can make a room, interior or vignette do the same thing using the evocative power of color.

As an artist I might have a heightened awareness of color, but all people seem to be drawn to certain color stories that

connect with their own personalities and life experiences. I describe my personal color story as *where the sea meets the shore*. Imagine the inside of a seashell: pearly greys, whites, creams, silvers, turquoise and delicate greens, with notes of slightly warmer tones such as blush, fawn and lavender.

In my particular aesthetic, cooler ethereal and watery tones are tempered with earthier grounded shades. Working with values of similar intensity and depth of tone yet layering in both warm and cool hues results in a very versatile and pleasing palette. Putting together a subtle mix of colors in the middle range (neither shades too dark nor pastels too light) brings depth and complexity to a color story, providing visual interest that is more soothing than the contrast of dark with light, or vibrant colors paired with white. With this approach, what at first might appear to be a monochromatic scheme will in fact have many nuances of color that come alive throughout the day as the light changes. You want to encourage a gentle flow. Within a soft, cohesive framework, I might introduce one accent color to prevent it from feeling too bland, or bring in a deeper, anchoring tone, but never with jarring contrasts.

I describe my personal color story as "where the sea meets the shore"— cooler watery tones tempered with earthy, grounded shades.

Not only is color evocative, it is also harmonizing, and certainly the most effective tool for unifying an environment. You can easily bring random and eclectic elements together just by choosing your palette thoughtfully. Lighter-colored schemes and neutral palettes bring out all the textures of a space and the objects within it and are the most forgiving for those who are not confident working with color or are having difficulty making a space feel pulled together.

I do understand that many people are drawn to more dynamic, charged colors. A shock of color can be fabulous in a piece of art or a striking pillow of Indian silks. Saturated hot pink in a tropical climate is amazing. A pop of rosy coral or Chinese red can be such a beautiful complement to a turquoise or sea-green palette. Generally, though, I feel a home environment is a place to feel peaceful and tranquil, and my color choices reflect this. I find fresh flowers are a lovely way to punctuate a space with color choices that can change with your moods and the seasons.

There are many ways to discover your own personal color story. You can study color theory, go to design school, work with color chips and color wheels—but the best way to learn about color is to play with different combinations, make your own inspiration boards, mix your own paints. I always say look to nature as a guide. Explore a garden, look at the forest floor and see how things are brought together. I am sure that spending my youth exploring the natural world heightened my own senses.

The most consistent compliment I have received in my years of working with paint, textiles and interiors is "You have a wonderful sense of color." Sense is really what it is all about . . . almost a sixth sense, an unspoken understanding of the influence of tones and shades, how they interplay, combine and resonate together. My work as a photographer is greatly influenced by my sensitivity to color and how I work with available light.

Terri Price in her blog *Windlost* so wonderfully described entering my space as "like waking up in a lovely, watery dream … The shop truly has the feeling of an underwater garden, inspired no doubt by Heather's upbringing on the coast and her love for all things natural."

When I first opened my shop, I thought I should include some items that veered from my own personal palette in an attempt to appeal to all tastes. In the end, I listened to my intuition and chose not to water it down (or fire it up, actually). Thanks to this decision, I have become known for my signature sense of color and for my nature-inspired collections and paintings. *House and Home* magazine described my shop as "a boutique dressed in driftwood hues."

Typically, when we refer to "natural colors" in design, we conjure visions of subtle, earthy shades. But, in truth, every color can be found in nature. There's an old saying: "Blue and green should not be seen without a color in between." How odd, I've always thought, when we see them together every day—when blue and green are

the colors of the sky, the grass, the sea and the flowers. More accurately, the neutral tones most often called "natural" tend to reflect the raw state of materials (such as wood or cloth) that have not been painted or dyed in artificial or garish colors. If you're challenged by color selection, a helpful start to creating an elegant palette is to work with tones close to the authentic shades of the materials you are working with in any given project.

For example, when I'm choosing wool, I gravitate toward winter whites, creams, greys and browns. I'm drawn to clay and ceramics in muted tones as opposed to bright, multicolored glazes. And I love glass in sheer bluey-green watery shades, like old shipwrecked bottles that have been sandblasted at the bottom of the sea. While I don't prefer rust as a paint tone, when occurring

authentically in materials such as eroded metals, old bricks and copper, it can be so rich and pleasing. I find it especially attractive when offset with the chalky tones found in grout, plaster and cement, and also with sea greens (think of copper with its gorgeous patina).

When choosing textiles and objects for decor, pay attention to the surfaces as well. Glossy, satin, matte, pebbled, velvety, dull, smooth—all these different surface choices affect the way a color reads. The "same" color scheme will look very different on an eggshell-finish paint chip, for example, than in a dupioni silk chosen for decorative pillows.

In addition to material and surface, you also have to think of light. Color, after all, is just reflected light bouncing back at us. Colors interact with the different times of day and year. Daylight can feel cool and flat on cloudy days, warm and saturated on sunny days. While ambient light can bring a toasty warm atmosphere that feels lovely and romantic, it can also shift colors in a way you may not have planned for.

I just adore light and airy spaces, painted white floors, French doors with sunlight

I painted a feature wall in my shop with Benjamin Moore Hazy Blue. It was so surprisingly versatile, I must've given out the paint shade a hundred times. My painting *Of Fog and Snow* echoes the tones in greyed-down versions.

flooding in. This look is dreamy for a beachy summer house. But light by itself is incomplete. We cannot have light without shadow. Shadow is what darkens the moon, offers shade and shelter for creatures, cools us down and allows for hibernation. In design and color selection, too, we need to include both light and shadow.

You can find many subtle ways of bringing depth into color pigments and interiors to provide the grounding quality of shadow. A room can be "greyed down" by using a little bit of a putty tone to provide strength and gravity. Or an old, weathered piece of furniture could be left with white paint flaking to reveal the earthy quality of the wood underneath. By working cleverly with shadow and light, you can suggest foreground and background, play up silhouettes, offset art and layer a space.

Every morning when I wake, I can't help but be enchanted by the way my sheer curtains allow the light to gently cascade into my bedroom. I have a rice-paper globe fixture overhead that makes me think of the sun and the moon. As the day unfolds and light moves across the room, orchids and candleholders create lyrical shadows upon my wall. Being attuned to the natural turning of light to dark, allowing time for exploration, then for quiet, rest and dormancy, is one of the great gifts (and struggles) of life. To deny one is to deny the other.

If you want a home that feels right for you, be true to your sense of color. Surround yourself with the colors that speak to you and heighten your sense of pleasure and peace. I know I'm just not very happy in a dark environment. I also know that certain colors lift my soul and inspire me. If you want a career in the visual arts, you need to also be sensitive to how color makes others feel.

Here are my favorite go-to colors, and why . . .

sea salt white

Purists who love only whites know that white is a palette unto itself, containing a myriad of shades with undernotes of cream, blue, lavender or even chartreuse. If you want a versatile white that does not compete with other colors, go for a pure white with just an ever-so-faint hint of grey—not too peachy or creamy. Old, faded linen sheets have this tone, as do ironstone china and the powdery patinas of zinc and plaster. This slightly cooler, sea salt tone also makes me think of the palest shade of bleached bone found in the desert, as well as oyster shells, seagull feathers, quartz and white pebbles.

White-on-white schemes beautifully highlight texture and form, but cool whites can sometimes look sterile. For a larger painted surface, I lean toward an ever-so-slightly warmer paint shade called Snowfall by Benjamin Moore. This chalky, clean white offsets the art and the other tones found in treasures throughout my boutique. As a trim or highlight, snow or bone white has a neutrality that highlights the delicate undertones of other shades.

white evokes
pure / clean

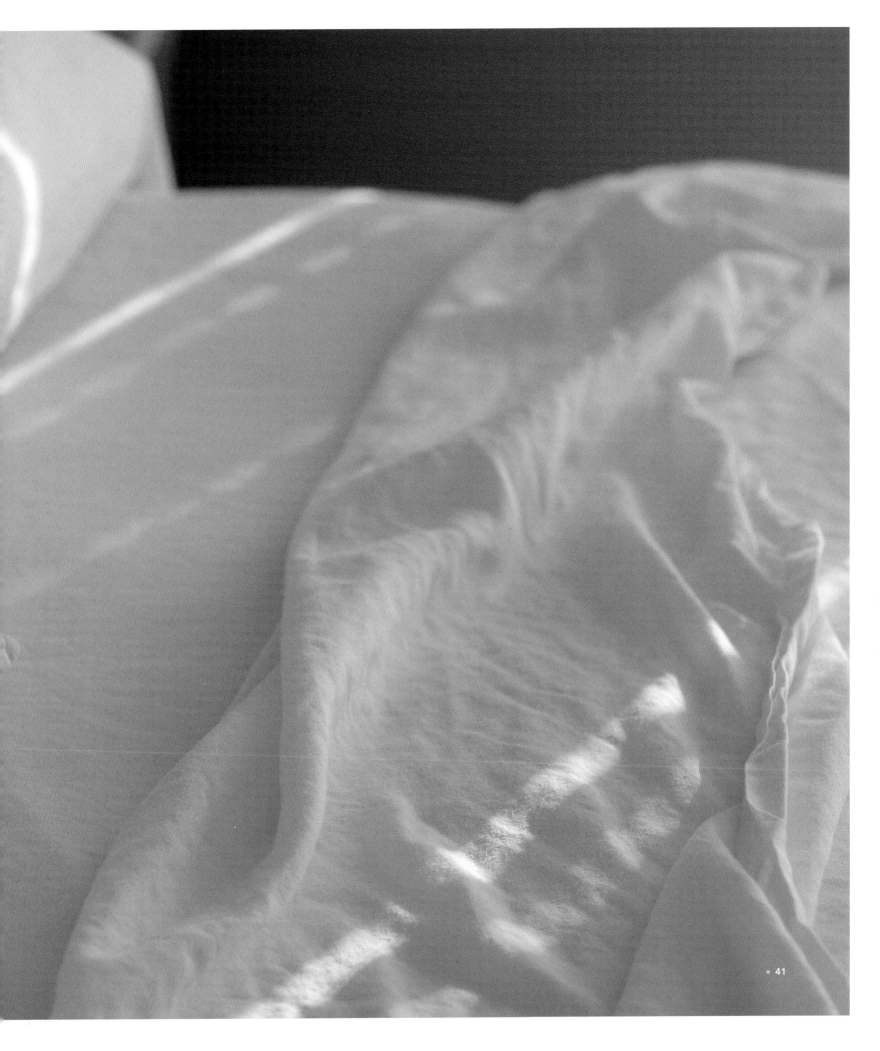

misty grey

Grey is timeless. Neither masculine nor feminine, it is cozy like a grey flannel coat, an elegant cat, a smoldering fire. It can be sexy and sophisticated, like a smoky eye. Down to earth like pebbles at the beach or an old, banged-up wash bucket. Imagine tarnished silver with its deep array of tones. A stormy sky holds a myriad of shades, from an almost-white misty haze to a deep, dark, moody grey on the underbelly of swollen clouds.

A slightly somber shade, grey is so lovely lightened up with tones of white and pale woods, evoking a Nordic palette of snow, stone and birch. Classic and timeless, think of the look of a fine grey cashmere sweater paired with a white shirt.

Shades of grey, pewter and charcoal have made their way into kitchens and bathrooms, with painted cabinetry, marble counters and oxidized metal hardware. Greyed oak is a wonderful choice for flooring, creating a neutral foundation for a home without casting a conflicting hue onto walls. It evokes the pale silvery facades of weathered barns.

Thick grey wool is a versatile material for felt accessories, knitted throws and braided poufs; sturdy and contemporary, yet soft and inviting, it brings a tactile depth to a space. Grey can feel gentle like a soft kitten or pussy willows, or soothing and enveloping like fog. On cloudy days I feel at peace cocooning with Earl Grey tea and cozy blankets.

grey evokes
quiet / soothing

shore

Imagine the shade of shallow water at the shore's edge, in an estuary where a stream meets the silty sea. Or a frothy ocean colored by grains of sand churned by the waves, diffused with light as the sun filters through to the ocean floor, echoing grey and blue from the sky above.

Shore is my signature color. A sandy blue green, it is distinguished by its milky quality with sophisticated greyed-down notes. I cannot explain why I am so captivated by this color. It instills a sense of peace within me. Its depth and complexity allow it to be both weighty and airy, and it feels right in any season. Found in French and Swedish antiques and interiors as a paint color, it can also be described as duck egg. A lovely choice for a serene bedroom dressed in layers of silk or linen, beautiful with tumbled stone or marble in a spa-like bathroom. A multitude of similar silvery blue greens can be found in the garden: succulents, cacti, dusty miller, sage, eucalyptus, beach grasses.

The celadon glaze that has adorned Asian ceramics for centuries imparts a similar pale jade tone. A slightly more glassy green, yet tinged with opacity, this delicate glaze has a translucent depth and clarity that reveals just a hint of the underlying clay, emulating the layers of sand and sea.

shore evokes
calm / serene

linen

Derived from flax, linen has a lovely oatmeal tone that is somewhere between grey and beige. Similar to the varying tones of driftwood, linen is perhaps the most perfect neutral, neither too gold nor too red. When I think of the elegant, rustic homes in France, I envision linen with worn stone and weathered beams.

You can never go wrong with linen as either a textile or a shade. An obvious fit for earthy palettes, this tone also makes a beautiful canvas for softer pastel shades such as petal pink, lilac and powder blue. Linen is also time-less and universal with crisp white.

A similar, slightly deeper shade I like to see in interiors could be described as twig brown. If you look at fine branches, you will often see little flecks of white on the nutty brown bark. Perhaps nature's version of "taupe"—imagine walnut shells, pinecones, papery dried leaves. I find the best way to bring these nutty, twiggy browns into a scheme is with wood itself.

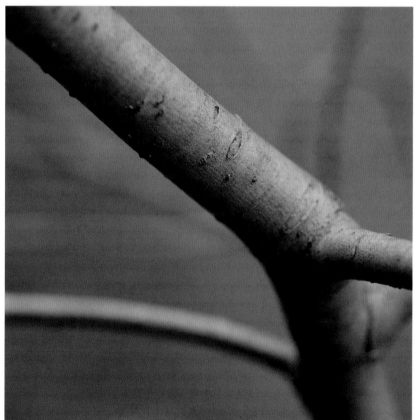

linen evokes
natural/elegant

mollusk blue

I scanned my mind to come up with the perfect word to describe this color. Glacial blue, Nordic blue, periwinkle, silvery blue did not capture its complexity. So I was delighted to settle upon mollusk after a day of beachcombing, for it perfectly captures the dreamy slightly mauve-blue tone found on mussel shells that also can range from the palest hint of greyish blue to a deeper, darker inky shade.

What sets this tone apart from the other blues I love is that it has no green undernotes. Ethereal, soothing and atmospheric, mollusk is a pleasing complement to darker chocolate tones. Not to be confused with sky blue, as you will find it only at dawn and twilight. Much more mature than baby blue, mollusk resides in the patina of blueberries and in hydrangea petals as they tinge with the arrival of autumn. Metals can often take on this tone in the iridescence of their patinas.

Mollusk blue's dreamy quality makes it ideal for bedrooms. Certain shades of natural indigo will take on this deep yet calming blue grey. As an artist, one of my favorite paints to work with is called Payne's grey. Named after a British watercolorist who used it as a more subtle alternative to grey, it is made with a mixture of crimson lake, raw sienna and indigo.

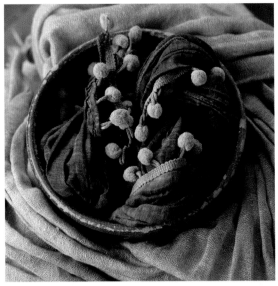  

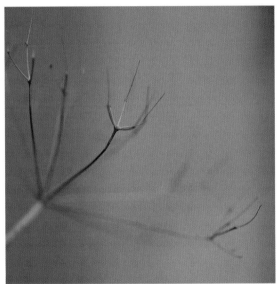  

mollusk blue
evokes
dreamy / peaceful

lavender

The one "warmer" color I truly adore and use consistently as an accent is the lovely and versatile lavender. The great thing about lavender is its ability to act as a neutral, mixing so well with greys, browns, taupe and creams, while also complementing other colors such as blues and greens. I've described it as "the new grey." One year I created a whole festive tableau in lavender, inspired by an amazing sea urchin shell I found that matched the tones of an old Tuscan pitcher with its rare glaze of dappled lilac. The sea urchin was an unusual choice, perhaps, but I peppered the scene with snowy whites and tarnished silvers to give it a glimmer.

I just love mixing lavender tones with natural raw linen. I painted my living room wall the palest tint of lavender, and it goes so beautifully with my drapes. My moldings are white, and you can't quite tell if there is color painted on the wall or just a warm, rosy bounce of light.

Lavender is the more mature, or masculine, version of pink. It has a gravity to it, yet is still undeniably pretty. The sophisticated depth of lavender is a fabulous choice to mix into an earthy palette. You might be surprised to discover how often lavender is found in nature. Not just in flowers, this tone surfaces like a velvety cloak on many natural forms. It elevates a still life or room to something beyond just "natural."

lavender evokes
tranquil / gentle

lichen and moss

These shades of green are distinguished by olivey-earthy notes with silvery or yellow undertones. Lichens can be pale, papery greens with greyish qualities, while moss can be much more verdant—yet both are the epitome of earthy greens. I lean more toward the lichen range, yet I do love mossy greens in pottery, garden rooms and, naturally, in plant material. Just one random lichen-encrusted branch makes a tactile addition to a tableau. I love to place undulating bits of lichen into bowls and glass vessels, and to fill the base of orchid planters with moss.

Within this family of greens is a hue I call peridot. A gemstone rather than a plant, peridot has a particular significance to me because it is my birthstone. This color can go from the clear, yellowy green of a shallow pond filled with new life to the young, tender shoots of bamboo. Not quite as sharp or acidic as chartreuse, peridot still has fresh verve. Distinguished by its clear-and-sheer quality, peridot is not muddy at all. Imagine the color of cats' eyes or a teeny tree frog shining like a jewel in the sun. It's gorgeous as a paint color for a sunroom, and I love it framed with glossy white trim or wainscoting. The softer celery tones of lichen and peridot also look beautiful in shimmering silks.

lichen and moss ...

evoke lively/earthy

sisal

The straw-like material of sisal, with its warm, wheaty tone, is actually derived from the agave plant, a great renewable resource. This buff color is a buttercream shade that brings the feeling of sunshine into a room without being as dominant as its stronger counterpart, yellow. This is an earthier ecru tone that blends beautifully with whites, is fresh with greens and is rich with soft browns.

Think natural fibers such as sea grass, twine, rope, string. As a flooring choice, sisal rugs with their rough, nubby weave bring an organic touch to a space. A functional and attractive way to store and display items is using baskets and bins woven out of reedy fibers; they look great row upon row on clean, white shelves in a bedroom or bathroom. I often find old painted furniture in a creamy shade that has become slightly more golden over the years. Beeswax and church candles with their wonderful almond or honey tones are another way to introduce this color, as an accent.

A. L. Nield, M.P.S.
DISPENSING CHEMIST
MANCHESTER ROAD, DENTON
LANCASHIRE
Telephone: DENton 2668

sisal evokes
sunshine / warmth

robin's egg blue

There is something so pure and joyful about robin's egg blue. Both uplifting and serene, it has universal appeal. Women love it in all its Tiffany-blue shades, children love its sweet Easter-egg quality, and everyone can relate to its special brilliance that evokes a clear summery sea. Robin's egg blue is also surprisingly versatile, perhaps because it is just slightly softer than turquoise and seems at once sheer and light yet also chalky and opaque. Robin's egg blue is beautiful with white, silver or gold, lovely offset against chocolate brown, dreamy with cream. It also works with many other shades of green and blue, as well as contrasted against opposing colors such as pale, muted yellow or coral.

The robin's egg itself represents life, birth, creation, nature, abundance, growth, innocence, springtime and purity. I find it to be both a perfect color and form. Who does not feel delight upon discovering a robin's egg safely tucked into a soft, earthy, twiggy nest?

Within the family of robin's egg blue, I love turquoise as an accent.

For interiors, I prefer turquoise not as deep or saturated as the semi-precious stone but more like a clear tropical sea. I painted a feature wall in my boutique with a shade called Hazy Blue. I intended to leave it just a few weeks, but it was such a gorgeous and surprisingly versatile color, I kept it for years. I must've given out the paint shade name to hundreds of customers.

robin's egg blue evokes
joyful / uplifting

seashell blush

Fleshy in tone, this is a sensual color found within the inner protected curve of a furling seashell. A faint, warm, pearly pink with caramel and toffee swirled in. With its undertones of beige, seashell blush is not sickly sweet but rather a very natural nude. A home with little notes of this gentle shade worked in as accents feels luxurious and soothing.

Mixed tone-on-tone with glossy white and pale woods such as birch, shell pink can give a feminine allure to things without being girly.

I also love to use flowers in these gentle warm tones both in interiors as cut flowers and in the garden, for they play beautifully off green and silvery foliage. Seashell blush can be introduced in small touches such as shell buttons, tea-stained ribbon, rose quartz and flowers such as peonies, Juliet roses and magnolias. At its deepest, blush might almost be a rosy coral, sweet ripe apricot or warm fawn brown shade.

Paired with shimmery decor, this color can be glamorous; grounded with beige, linen and café au lait browns, it can feel very natural. I find it especially exquisite layered in textiles of varying surfaces such as shiny silks and fluffy mohair.

seashell blush evokes
sensual / feminine

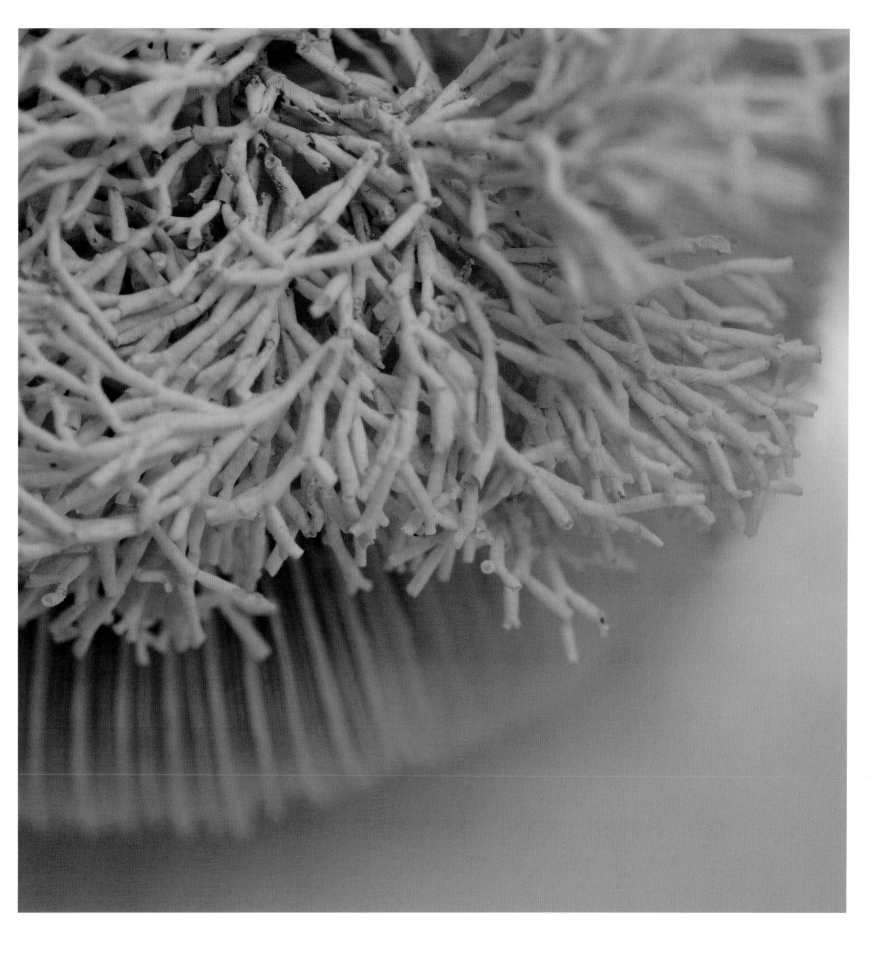

4

vignettes and the art of placing

I'VE ALWAYS USED the term *vignette* to describe my small displays and assemblages of finds. Vignetting seems to be part of my own personal vernacular, so I want to offer a thorough exploration of how I bring things together in this *art of placing*. In styling, a vignette tells a story using objects instead of words. In the same way an author puts together words or a painter combines color and movement, we can create lyrical beauty with objects. Using a mindful approach, we can elevate the art of placement to poetry. So, think of each object as a word in a poem or haiku; choose them thoughtfully and bring them together artfully.

While researching for this book, I was rather charmed to learn that the root form of the word *vignette* comes from the French word *vigne*, referring to the decorative vine garlands found at the front of a book or chapter. In a literary sense, vignette also refers to an evocative description so brief that, metaphorically, it could be written on a vine leaf.

When I brought this
fragile book of botanicals
home from a Paris market,
my cat nestled himself in
to the still life.

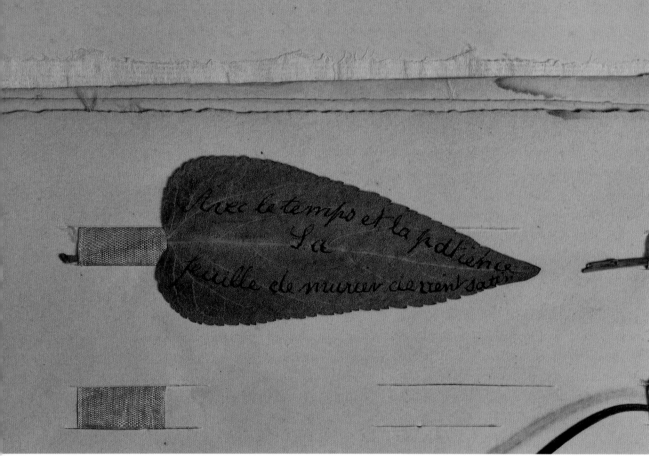

In a literary sense, vignette
refers to an evocative
description so brief it can
be written on a vine leaf.

This reminds me of one of my most beloved treasures, a late-nineteenth-century book with pressed botanicals and a few leaves that have been carefully scripted by hand in just this manner and woven into its fragile pages.

In my boutique, people often remark on how I bring seemingly disparate finds together in a way that feels connected and pleasing. I always consider the *alchemy* I am creating when bringing objects together. With thoughtful intention, using the *natural eclectic* philosophy as a guide, you can juxtapose a diverse range of elements and forms in such a way that a vignette feels natural and interesting. Be mindful that an

eclectic look is not simply random items haphazardly plunked together.

The art of placement requires thought as well as ways of seeing that may be new to you. A poetic vignette depends upon how the objects work together to delight the eye and the mind, and to tell a little story. It also depends on how the curves, linear forms and spaces between the objects resonate together as a group. The key is to think about a vignette as a harmonious whole.

Approach it like a painter would create a still life. Traditionally, artists would set up small arrangements with objects of varying characteristics that would showcase the artist's ability to

render them in a painting. Compositions would capture three-dimensional shapes such as fruits, the delicate, detailed forms of flowers, the drape and folds of cloth, and reflective surfaces such as silver. When photography was introduced, artists continued to use still lifes as a way to capture shadow, light and form on film.

In an artful home, we can create displays and vignettes in much the same way. The French term for still life is *nature morte*, which translates literally to "dead nature"; but a vignette or still life need never feel static, or lacking life. Drift-wood, moss, pinecones, bare branches, sprigs in bloom—all can contribute to a vignette that is alive, tactile and transformative. You can keep the foundation of a grouping the same and intro-duce elements from outdoors with the turn of the seasons. Flowers in your arrangement will unfold, bloom, fade and be replaced or left in their varying phases of decay. You may place a cherished new memento amongst your favorite treasures or subtract an element as it loses its charm. Natural finds will each have their own unique thumbprint. No two pebbles, no two branches will ever be identical. This is the magic of nature. So let us think of still life as *captured* rather than *unchanging*.

Always consider the alchemy you are creating when bringing objects together for a vignette. With thoughtful intention you can juxtapose a diverse range of elements so that they resonate as a harmonious whole.

With fresh eyes, choose the ingredients for a vignette as if you're inventing a new recipe. Expand your visual vernacular and select items rich in form and texture to create a certain chemistry.

Choose the ingredients for vignettes with fresh eyes, as if you are inventing a new recipe. Aim for a certain chemistry with items that resonate together and create a new cohesive whole (just as you combine ingredients in baking to create something greater than the sum of their parts).

Try to expand your visual vernacular. Consider a bowl, for example: the shape, color, form, density. Is it shiny, smooth or rough? Geometric or organic in shape, small or large? Is it transparent, opaque, dark, light? Now, let's look at a vase. Is it curvy, linear, delicate, chunky, old, new? Is the material glass, metallic, ceramic, wood? What are you going to put it on—a stack of books, a tray, pedestal, pillow, hatbox?

You can connect objects in different ways. For example, you could place a simple white vase beside a white seashell, joining them simply by their *color*. As discussed in my color chapter, I tend to create groupings that are within a single color family or that meld two color stories together, interweaving objects related by tone and form. Taking it further, you could place that same seashell next to a white vase that is scalloped like an oceanic form, setting them both on a stack of books about the ocean. You now have the further connections of form and an ocean theme in addition to the monochromatic white palette. You can work with *harmonies of related themes*, such as botanical, ethnic, and flora and fauna. Or you can create a vignette *inspired by*

This harmonious vignette is connected not only by the white-on-white palette but also by the beachy oceanic themes.

Look beyond the objects themselves to the outlines, shapes and negative spaces formed between the objects. The silhouettes of teapots and pitchers are especially pleasing, with the enclosed shape of their handles creating a peek-a-boo.

materials; for example, mixing an old zinc lantern with a mercury glass vase on a silver tray creates harmony with the elemental metallic qualities.

To prevent the aesthetic of the vignette from appearing bland, I might add one or two elements of surprise. It is the choosing of this "random" outside element that really makes a vignette special. You can create opposites and contrasts with interesting juxtapositions, offsetting opaque against transparent, soft and fuzzy textures against glassy and smooth, round against blocky.

When I create a vignette, I also look beyond the objects themselves to the spaces, outlines and shapes formed between the objects. This "negative space" is actually something very positive to

consider when composing anything in the visual arts, and it applies to styling as well.

Imagine you have two rectangular vases side by side with a gap between. The space between them would essentially feel the same: a straight-sided space. But if you put a trophy beside a straight-sided vase, all of a sudden you have an interesting shape between the two items. Consider teapots and pitchers, such lovely forms with their handles and spouts. The handle is curvilinear, which both draws the eye *and* creates an enclosed shape—a peekaboo through which we can see things. What do we see within this window of space, this opening? It depends on what you choose to place behind it! Layering objects with different silhouettes, pulling items forward and backward, you can create a myriad

You can see here the evolution of a vignette as I layer and add forms until I find just the right balance and rhythm.

I like to bring together treasures for their own specific charm as opposed to a shared historical period. Consider this the eclectic aspect of a vignette.

Look for items
with finishes
that complement
each other so as
not to create a
distracting jumble.

of spaces and shapes, not just with the objects themselves but with these negative spaces.

The trick is to gauge the right amount of space so things feel neither crowded nor disconnected—have some fun and play around with it until it feels just right. You want some variety in height and length and width, but not so much that you distract the eye with elements that are out of proportion with the others.

I LIKE TO combine treasures chosen for their own specific charm as opposed to a shared historical period. Mixing *new with old* and bringing things together from different periods is what keeps vignettes fresh, original and timely. Think of this as the eclectic aspect of vignetting. When choosing furnishings and objects from different eras, look for items with finishes that complement each other so you don't just create a distracting jumble.

Throughout my photographs in this book, you will see texture and patina everywhere—so much so that I decided I didn't need to dedicate a chapter to this subject. I find it especially effective to offset objects with richly nuanced patina and textural appeal against flatter, smoother objects and surfaces. Glossy-white lacquered or molded plastic and resin furniture, smooth painted walls, marble counters and glazed tiles and ceramics provide a lovely contrast and backdrop to show off patina. One of the reasons old items hold such charm for me is the way they take on their own unique finish and surface, much like a human face, becoming truly one of a kind.

Find out what you love most (and why), and start collecting those things for the joy they bring you. Here are some of *my* treasured objects, things that bring me joy. Notice how I've worked them into a variety of scenarios throughout the pages of this book.

glass

I love glass that is slightly misshapen or handblown with subtle irregularities. A group of transparent objects can be especially alluring, with light shining through and playing off the interacting forms. Layering glass vessels in different tones creates new shades, adding visual interest without being too demanding or distracting to the eye. Old bottles come in so many fabulous shapes and forms, some with long, curved necks, others with subtle graphics (letters or words) printed into them.

Glass is such a wonderful prop for a photographer because its luminous quality translates light so beautifully. The distortions in thick glass and curvilinear forms can add visual interest, magnifying other objects, inverting reflections, casting remarkable transparent shadows and refractions.

I'm attracted to old glass fishing floats for similar reasons. While glass seems like such a fragile material, it is surprisingly sturdy when it's perfectly round and filled with air. These blown-glass spheres have been crafted in Asia from recycled glass for over a century. Knotted to fishing nets to keep them afloat, some broke free and were carried by ocean currents to our west coast. Imagine their journeys before drifting up onto our shores! My grandparents lived on the coast of Vancouver Island where floats would wash up on the beach. My parents scattered them on our cabin deck in Halfmoon Bay; they would be familiar tones of blue and green, as well as root-beer brown and even amethyst.

The floats with netting still intact feel like perfect little examples of craft, with their hand-knotted string and twine, some showing signs of small *wabi-sabi* repairs where the netting had frayed, or with bits of algae or barnacles still clinging to the netting. I love to group bunches of fishing floats together in bowls or feature a particular gem as a highlight in a still life. They truly are one of my most treasured finds.

silvered surfaces

Of all the metals, I prefer silver. To me, tarnish is not a blight or detriment but rather an alluring reflective quality of iridescence and depth. You can find fabulous silver forms as pitchers, water jugs, trophies and urns, and use them as vases or vessels for small plants such as succulents. In a bedroom or bathroom, silver trays make a lovely base for a vignette of perfume bottles, jewelry and keepsakes.

Authentic old mirrors are hauntingly beautiful when the silvering starts to erode and create organic peeling and rusting patterns within the glass, where part of it becomes transparent and the rest remains reflective.

Mercury glass is striking for its crackling and shimmering tonalities. I'm often asked what I like to collect and, I must say, I'm just crazy for old mercury-glass Christmas ornaments. I like the simple, round, solid-colored baubles in which the metallic surface inside the glass has started to craze and create little bubbly patterns. Authentic old mercury-glass vessels and ornaments are no longer easy to find, but this is one of the few things that can be nearly as charming in new reproduction versions.

books

Not surprisingly, I love books—for their covers, for the stories they contain, for their graphics. Stacks of books create great platforms for displays. Antique and vintage books can have leather or linen-bound covers embossed with beautiful metallic text and ornamentation. Often too fragile to handle, such books with their faded covers are like little works of art that can be used simply for display. You can find wonderful old paper in the pages inside printed with gorgeous old engravings, often with quaint sayings that represent the time in which they were written. Many books have charming designs and motifs on their spines that are visually appealing layered one above the other. When I use books in my displays, I consider not only their color and material but also the content of the book and how it relates to the theme of a vignette.

coral, shells, ocean motifs

The number of graceful forms that come from the sea is almost incomprehensible. Sand dollars bearing soft tracings of flower-like motifs. Sea urchin shells with their perfectly radiating dotted surfaces. Conch shells with their spirals. Coral in all its lacy, undulating glory. These delicate forms so beautifully complement almost any arrangement. Large clamshells and abalone shells make beautiful shallow vessels that can be filled with other natural elements.

The ways these ocean forms can be used is endless. Just be sure to collect ocean treasures in a way that keeps our oceans and sea creatures alive for centuries to come. (For more on ethical foraging, see my closing chapter.)

birds' nests, feathers, eggs

Nests represent shelter, eggs new life. I adore nests for both their symbolism and their tactile quality. If I find a nest that has fallen from a tree in a storm or is clearly long abandoned, then I might keep and cherish it. The "nests" I've purchased for my shop are plant fiber molded into a soft form evocative of a nest. I've gathered dried plant waste from the community gardens a block from my home and emulated this look by winding feathery, dried, grassy, rooty materials together.

Feathers come in such an array of shapes, colors, patterns and textures. Soft and downy, shiny and iridescent, striped or graduated, a randomly found feather can look lovely placed in a vase, resting on a book or tucked into a basket.

Strong yet fragile, eggs are one of the most perfect forms ever created. From tiny speckled quail eggs to large creamy ostrich eggs, they are perfect symbols of new life to use in your displays. Some, such as emu eggs and Araucana chicken eggs, come in an array of gentle blue-green tones. Eggs made of marble, glass, wood or even papier-mâché make charming props as well.

orchids and succulents

Fresh-cut flowers are a beautiful addition to any space. Potted orchids are my mainstay though, for their timeless elegance, enduringly abundant blooms and gently arcing stems. They bring a lyrical quality to a vignette and add an exotic air to an interior. Whereas the foliage on common houseplants can sometimes look neglected, dusty and forlorn over time, orchids put on a graceful show for months on end.

Playful, small plant containers are also attractive to use as a live focal point. Terrariums and succulents have made quite a comeback. In particular, I love the graphic concentric form of the *Echeveria* group of cacti, which can look quite Zen when isolated in simple little pots. Their silvery greens come in all sorts of hues ranging from a lilac tone to pale brown or grey. They can bring living energy into the home in such a quaint and humble way.

ironstone china and creamware

The pure form of white ceramics makes them an unbeatable choice for any home. Gorgeous whether lined up on a kitchen shelf, placed individually on a bedside table or displayed in an old armoire. Pitchers, mugs and teacups with their charming handles, old ironstone china, pudding bowls in incremental sizes all in a row—you just can't go wrong with these simple forms. They bring quiet to an arrangement and offset the more decorative qualities of other treasures. The silhouettes of lidded casseroles and spouted gravy boats look so enticing layered together on a kitchen pantry shelf. Elegant and sophisticated or casual and beachy, creamware vessels also look gorgeous filled with seashells and ocean treasures in all their chalky, pearly tones.

chinoiserie and asian ceramics

While living in France, I was captivated by the flair the French have for mixing simple, Provençal furnishings with decorative Asian objects. European expeditions to the Orient from the sixteenth to nineteenth centuries greatly influenced European styles, inspiring the French word *chinoiserie* that describes this look.

A little touch of Asian influence adds another layer of complexity and sophistication to an interior. Decoratively appealing prints can be found in textiles and china patterns, featuring lyrical cherry blossom branches, stylized urns, and bamboo and bird motifs. Asian ceramic vessels, ginger jars and tea bowls range from exquisitely ornate to primitive and pure in form. I covet rustic ginger jars in bisqued clay and jade tones; they look fabulous grouped together en masse. I also collect blanc de chine statuettes and figurines of the goddess Kwan Yin, as she holds a special meaning for me.

5

create,
capture and
captivate

I LOVE SEEING THE current upswing in handmade artisanal goods and thriving cottage industries. I come from a crafting background myself. At the age of fifteen I started knitting and selling one-of-a-kind sweaters. Made with hand-spun yarns and my own handmade ceramic buttons, the sweaters had wonderful heathered tones and a nice nubby texture similar to the chunky infinity scarfs we see today.

My mentor was Mary, a schoolmate's mother, who wove rugs on a large loom that stood on a brick floor, surrounded by windows overlooking a garden. I was captivated by all the texture and rusticity—hints of moss had crept indoors onto the old bricks. Mary taught me how to spin wool and make natural dyes. I would create a great witch's brew on our kitchen stove with bits of bark and lichen and use it to dye my wool. The hands-on process spoke to me so much that I would happily toil for hours over my creations.

Thankfully, I discovered not only did I love to create things, I loved to sell them too! And thus a life of being both a maker and a merchant began.

I truly was a young entrepreneur. Orders started rolling in based on the first sweater I ever knit and wore myself (this was long before Etsy, pop-up shops or the Internet). By my early twenties, I expanded my wares into a successful product line of hand-painted fabrics, bed linens and accessories that sold across Canada through interior designers and home-decor boutiques. While I regret not taking images of my early knitted creations (I used no patterns and no two were ever the same), I did have the business savvy to start creating an attractive portfolio of my

Whether spinning wool, creating original textile designs, painting freehand on cloth, or stitching up antique fabrics and trims into collage-style pillows, I've always loved working with textiles.

printed textiles with the handy Pentax K1000 I'd been carrying around with me since a young teenager.

Years later I moved to Paris, discovering so much inspiration in the old architecture, the narrow streets with charming old facades and, of course, the antique markets! During the day I worked as a "stylist," designing fabric patterns for a textile firm, and at night I taught myself to sew, so I could incorporate antique trimmings found at the markets into my creations. Using the beauty of my French apartment as a backdrop, I staged charming settings to photograph my latest collections. I had actually moved to Paris with a fashion photographer and gleaned a fair

bit about the trade through osmosis. I dabbled in the makeshift darkroom of our tiny kitchen, assisted on most shoots and immersed myself in the industry.

As serendipity would have it, when I returned to Vancouver in the early nineties to start life over, the strength of the photographs in my textile portfolio landed me my first professional photo shoot and opened the door to a flourishing new career. I took my folio in to the editor of a publication to promote the collections of pillows I'd created while living in France. An hour later I walked out the door with an invitation from the art director to shoot for their magazine! I was over the moon with excitement: my first paid

shoot ever would be for one of Canada's leading shelter magazines. This "new" work would bring all my varied experiences together. Without any formal training in the industry, I began not only shooting but also producing, styling and sometimes writing full-length features for publications.

I attribute much of my early success to knowing how to present my wares. Even then, I knew that it's not enough to make beautiful things; you also have to reach people with your work. I remember the buzz created by that meeting in the magazine's office. I had brought slides depicting lively antique markets, along with my well-curated portfolio of images and some tactile examples of my designs. Everyone gathered around, excited by what I was sharing. This is what it's about. Engaging people. Although this is much easier to do today, with

the Internet, competition is steeper. With so much online marketing, if you don't make a moving statement with your work, you'll get lost in the shuffle.

These days, with our plethora of digital cameras and phone devices, almost anyone can take up photography, but the trick is to make magical images. I know firsthand that if you want exposure for your goods (or your design skills), you need to know how to make displays with visual impact *and* capture them in their best light with fantastic photographs.

It can be costly to hire a professional photographer and stylist, but the results can be well worth it. I've been fortunate to be a maker, stylist and photographer, so I've done it all myself for years. For all you crafters, makers, thrifters and DIY stylists, this chapter is filled with my insider tips on how to style for craft sales, retail displays,

Art & Authentic

pop-up shops, blogs and photo shoots (with some simple, helpful tips on taking photos too!).

We've all been to fairs where crowds of people are cloistered around one display while passing right by others. Why do some booths barely earn a glance? In part, it's because the display has not been set up to make people want to see and learn more. Let's look at some of the elements that make for an inviting setting, whether it's in a craft market, a retail space or even your home.

First of all, you can make a display feel unique and alive by adding live elements such as florals, fresh fruit and greenery. Bring in natural textiles too, to add softness and texture, instead of synthetic white or black banquet tablecloths, which look generic and dated. Use original art or atmospheric visuals as a backdrop to personalize the space and help set a mood. As I suggest in

the vignettes chapter, create interconnectedness between the objects you're displaying. Also, think about how the space, booth or table display is framed; use all of the surfaces to create a cohesive, dynamic space so it doesn't feel like just a table in a box. If you're merchandising small items that are all the same size, elevate them with added props that can work as a backdrop. Funky old ladders, benches, trunks and chests can double as storage and give you a variety of surfaces and heights to work with. Beware of creating a jumble of visual stimulation, though. Your wares will benefit if you allow for some quiet in your display, just as antiques and art often show off better amidst the clean, modern lines of a spacious gallery than in a dark, cluttered Victorian home.

If you're creating retail displays, you also want to think of visual flow—to imagine

Lacy forms such as large
birdcages, chandeliers
and charming old chairs
and little tables look great
stacked up in a window.
You can place tactile
treasures in or on them
to entice onlookers to
explore up close.

how the customer will move through and experience the space as a whole and how their eye will move from one display to another. Consider how closely people can interact with the merchandise. When curating my boutique, I always stand back to take in the whole view from the front entrance (like an artist assessing a work in progress), imagining how a new customer might experience the space for the first time.

For objects that are high up or on a backdrop wall, keep the shapes bold and strong. To display finer, delicate objects close up in a way that feels engaging, place them in a little cabinet or on a shelf with other small, precious treasures. I create small feature areas that are intimate

wholes, often containing a grouping within a certain color family to help distinguish it from other feature areas. I want each grouping to feel complete in itself, yet I am also mindful of the entire space working together.

You can be more fanciful and dramatic in shop displays than in a personal interior, so have some fun. The window display is where you really want to make a statement. Think of it as a stage. You want to capture attention with some bold strokes and props, yet also have some enchanting details that make viewers want to press their nose against the glass to see more. I like to create thematic windows, choosing props with eye-catching silhouettes.

SCALE AND DISPLAY

For objects that are high up or on a backdrop wall, keep the shapes bold and strong. To display finer, delicate objects close up in a way that feels engaging, place them in a little cabinet or on a shelf with other small, precious treasures.

KEEP IT CLEAN
Your wares will benefit if you allow for some quiet in your display, just as antiques and art often show off better amidst the clean, modern lines of a spacious gallery than in a dark, cluttered Victorian home.

The key to both showing and shooting merchandise is to tell a story your customers want to immerse themselves in and re-create in their own lives. Often, when new customers come in to my shop, they say, "I've driven by so many times, seen your lovely window displays and always wanted to come in." My boutique is next to a delightful bakery. I chuckle at the nose prints and delicate pastry crumbs greeting me at the doorstep each day. I just imagine the delighted faces as they eat their flaky croissants while peering into my shop!

So now that you've got your display set up or you've decorated a space you want to share or blog about, how do you capture it in equally beautiful photographs? While experimenting is the best way to learn photography, I'll offer you my favorite tips to get you started.

The principle of decluttering is as essential in photography as in editing a display. Not everything that looks great to the eye will read well in photos. Small things get lost from a distance or in wide shots, and the perspective can change how things appear. Spaces between objects may get compressed, so you may need to nudge some objects farther apart and group others closer together or remove them. You have to look through the lens and tweak! When I shoot homes for magazines, I spend most of my styling time removing little things scattered everywhere. I always find it remarkable to see the transformation of a home after accessories have been grouped and culled.

Little compositions like these create such charming focal points—and make for wonderful images to share on sites like Instagram.

With your smaller items, like vases, bottles and candles, go for graphic repetition to lead the eye and create rhythm. You can also contain collections of little found treasures en masse within transparent vessels, as an elegant and clutter-free way to show them off. Create focal points with floral groupings. Use large bowls filled with organic forms such as apples, stones, eggs or glass spheres to offset architectural lines in a scene. The idea is to pare things down so you can create areas of heightened visual interest. Invest in a great piece of original art that speaks to you; it can elevate and anchor a space. Bring in texture with chunky throws and pillows.

You don't need expensive cameras or fancy lighting to capture great images. To really master photography, though, you do need to develop an artful eye. The best way is to practice, hone your eye and learn to understand how light and composition read in an image. It is the photographer, not the equipment, that makes stunning photos!

I used only natural and available light for all the images in this book. You can get amazing results with just a simple white foam-core board to help bounce and reflect light into a scene. Contrary to popular opinion, you can also shoot *into* the light as long as you compensate and adjust your exposure so the backlit subject matter is properly exposed and not just in shadow. Backlit photos can have an especially dreamy quality due to the way the light refracts. Flowers, with their delicate transparent petals, are gorgeous

Flowers with their transparent petals
are captivating when photographed
backlit, as are other sheer items such
as textiles and glass.

GROUP AND GATHER

Create visual punctuation with floral groupings and large bowls filled with organic forms to offset the architectural lines within a scene. Bring in texture with chunky pillows and throws.

FOCAL POINT

Shooting with a "shallow depth of field" creates the effect of a background or foreground that softly melts away. The goal is to captivate the viewer by drawing the eye to a specific element. Don't just hold up your camera and click on a scene without focusing on the most interesting aspect.

when photographed this way, as are other sheer items such as textiles and glass.

One easy but very important photography tip I always share has to do with the focal point. Think of how, when we listen to someone speak, we filter out the background noise. We do the same when we focus on a subject with our eyes. We do not see everything clearly within our field of vision; this would be too much information for the brain to take in. Having everything in equally sharp focus is what I call "catalogue-style" photography. It looks unnatural to me because it's not true to how we actually experience three-dimensional spaces. It serves a purpose if you need to show all of a product in one shot or if you're shooting for a real-estate listing, but otherwise it can lack mood and atmosphere.

I prefer photographs that emulate the way the human eye sees, so I almost always shoot with a "shallow depth of field," which means opening up the aperture of a camera to an f-stop of 5.6 or lower. This lets in more light but also creates the effect of a background or foreground that falls off softly in focus.

This technique is especially effective and dreamy when shooting products up close, and applies to nature photography as well. You may want to highlight a butterfly on a flower, for example, and let the rest of the image melt away. It's also a great way to obscure distracting details or unattractive elements within a scene.

Images can be easily manipulated after the fact with software or apps, such as tilt shift in Instagram, to achieve a similar spot-focus look. However, I caution against applying an overall treatment without thought to composition; this can look gimmicky. Like heavy-handed makeup, overworked photos can be off-putting, so practice achieving a subtle, natural effect. The goal is to make an image that draws the eye to its most interesting aspect so as to captivate the viewer.

Remember to bring your own unique personality, perspective and imagination to all you do, so you don't get lost in a sea of ordinariness. By creating your own special atmosphere and capturing it beautifully, you will enchant others with your work.

6

a sense of place

As BOTH A photographer and a shopkeeper, I've been
fortunate to meet many kindred spirits who share
a love of beauty and authentic living. I've had the
pleasure of shooting some of their remarkable places and
spaces, collaborating with them to create stunning scenes
for editorial publication. As a photographer, I've traveled and
worked internationally, exploring many exciting locations
and homes.

In this chapter I'm sharing some special places dear to
my heart, some of which I've been fortunate enough to stay
at while traveling on assignment. It is so nice to break bread
together, share stories and get to know people in their homes.
To sleep in a comfy new bed as a houseguest, wake up to the
mood of the day, have the pleasure of walking around a property, exploring the local area, the gardens, the atmosphere—
this all adds to my experience. With a greater understanding

121

of who dwells in the places I shoot, I can bring an increased enthusiasm and sensitivity to the project.

I'm not one to show up with sets of lights, cables and reflectors when I do a photo shoot. Rather, I arrive with arms draped in textiles and branches, baskets of seashells, bottles and baubles in tow. I cull from my boutique, from whatever I can find in local sources and from nature walks. During the shoot, I work with the best elements within a home and add, subtract and layer to create the perfect atmosphere for an image. Then I let the mood of the day, the available light, and the personality of the home and those who live in it shine through.

I am deeply influenced by my surroundings, which you can see from the journal entry on the right written upon my arrival at Ebb Tide, the first location I profile in this chapter. When we truly take the time to explore new environments, we can feel stimulated and inspired rather than agitated, distracted or overwhelmed. Each of the spaces featured in this chapter has its own signature style, its own personal thumbprint and special sense of place created by the residing designers and homeowners.

On a very foggy January day, I boarded a ferry to a seaside cottage that was generously offered by friends to allow some quietude and shelter to work on the book. The gentle shroud of the day, the sea . . . and knowing I was leaving the urban distractions behind . . . these things instilled in me a feeling of peace and calm before I even arrived. Twilight was setting upon us, and there was the thinnest line of bright sky above the sea in between the water and the fog as darkness was setting in. It pulled at the artist in me and made me feel like painting. It was so striking, graphic and captivating. Upon entering the delightful cabin, I shifted moods from calm, peaceful and relaxed to inspired and stimulated. Despite being rather familiar with the home (I had previously photographed it for a magazine), it was like discovering it all over again. We lit a fire and took it all in. The bespoke items, hand-hewn surfaces, the personal treasures and special creative touches called out to me to explore. The stitching of a cotton quilt. A little handmade book bound within a clamshell. The smooth alluring surface of a pebbled bathroom floor.

I settled into a delightful frame of mind that was stimulated yet serene, filled with anticipation of what the morning horizon might bring. How the light might feel as it entered through the glassy seaside frontage . . . how my day would unfold as I wrote, captured images and explored the natural coastal setting. The removal of distraction, the exposure to the ever-changing elements outdoors, and the discovery of the artistic objects inside all deeply contributed to how I felt. Tension melted. Tranquility arrived.

ebb tide

You can see peppered throughout this book images that I captured while using Ebb Tide and its environs as a form of "daylight studio." Situated on the Sunshine Coast of British Columbia, this new build replaced an old cottage, yet it retains the charm and vintage feel of a cabin passed down through generations. Designed by the clever and resourceful homeowner Lara Irwin, it's a special place with many unique and playful notes.

Upon entering, you are greeted by a graphic octopus print hung with metal chains over a striking double-height Balinese stone fireplace, and you know this is not a predictable nautical escape. An old schoolhouse locker, exposed-beam joinery and raw materials bring in some industrial touches, while vintage signage found on Etsy.com adds whimsy. A collection of natural motifs and curiosities are displayed throughout. Inventive collages made by Lara punctuate the walls. Small touches include the handwritten tags labeling vintage mason jars upon the shelves. In the kitchen, mix-and-match silverware, raw wood surfaces and open shelving juxtapose the clean white subway tiles.

Ebb Tide delights the senses and feeds the imagination, allowing for the many friends and family of Rick and Lara Irwin to just relax and take it all in. The use of enduring materials is evident throughout. Nothing is excessive; everything is well thought out and of utmost quality. Wonderful textiles, Alaskan hand-scraped, fumed and oiled oak floors, brushed metal hardware, carefully executed moldings. Old zinc

nautical light fixtures. Hudson's Bay blankets in the bedroom layered upon crumply linens.

On warm nights dining on the expansive outdoor patio, you can smell the salt air and watch the sun drop down as it casts a rosy hue on the beach grasses. The ocean is just steps away, so you hear its thundering lull. Birds intentionally drop seashells from the air, and eagles cry from the trees above. I love the palette of oxidized metals, bleached woods and stone. The groupings of birds' nests, jars filled with feathers, maps of the sea and charts of the moon all acknowledge this cottage's place in the natural world.

With tiny details like vintage oceanic stamps carefully placed in a clamshell book, and grand gestures such as hand-scraped fumed oak floors throughout, Lara Irwin has infused Ebb Tide with charming bespoke touches.

italian farmhouse

My sister, Janet, lived in Italy for many years, including the time when I lived in Paris. The cobblestone streets, fields of poppies and groves of old olive trees around her home would call to me on my many visits to her over the years. We'd meander through quaint and colorful markets and pick up fresh artichokes and figs. We'd pick wild asparagus in the fields and get buckets of olives and dine al fresco. Days would be filled with walks on the clay-like earth, cutting through fields, taking in the gorgeous pastoral setting and visiting quaint neighboring villages. We'd go antiquing for my boutique, and then we'd lay out all the treasures on her terrace to behold. Summers would be нот. I loved being able to dine outside every night after these long days of exploration.

My sister's Italian home embraced warm, blushy tones: terra-cotta tiles, stone, plaster, wood. It was all about earthy texture and patina. A very rustic, old stone structure with exposed beams and a horse in the barn underneath. This sort of history, weightiness and rusticity you could not fake, though my sister did hand-stain the old plaster walls herself in ethereal layered hues. The interior was quite raw and eclectic—draped shawls, random furnishings, lots of candles—with modern Italian touches in the kitchen and bathroom. I'd always wanted to live on a farm surrounded by animals and bucolic vistas, so gathering warm, fawn-brown eggs from

her chickens amidst the sweet straw smell of horse and hay was very comforting to me.

This space looked out upon vineyards and fields of sunflowers. At night we'd light the fire in the deep, traditional fireplaces and catch up on life. Spending time with my sister (who now lives close by in Canada) would warm my heart and make me feel at home, in her home.

My sister's Italian home embraced warm, blushy tones: terra-cotta tiles, stone, plaster, wood. This sort of history, weightiness and rusticity you could not fake, though Janet did hand-stain the old plaster walls herself in ethereal layered hues.

I'd often seek out textiles and tapestries while in Europe. I had draped this tapestry from the top-floor window to allow it to freshen *en plein air* before packing it when, in true feline fashion, my sister's adorable cat, Angel, came to sit upon it like a queen on her throne.

haiku mill

Haiku Mill is both exotic and poetic. Located near the relaxed boho-surf town of Paia on the island of Maui, this lushly decaying old stone sugar mill has been transformed into an intoxicatingly beautiful location for weddings. Dripping with romantic flourishes, blossoming vines and glimmering chandeliers, this is a magical place for anyone who loves nature and fine European antiques.

Owner Sylvia Hamilton Kerr has brought in grand gestures throughout the tropical grounds, with antique French architectural elements, decorative ironwork and rustic finds. With the help of her sister, accomplished interior designer Nina Hamilton, Sylvia has brought the multiple indoor and outdoor structures on this sweeping property back to life. Both sisters grew up in Canada and still retain a strong connection to a coastal lifestyle, whether on a Hawaiian island or the coast of British Columbia. They have quite the eye for beauty, with a relaxed style that is inviting and engaging.

The main house is opulent with precious antique finds, yet also grounded in an earthiness, with all its beautiful terra-cotta tile work, antique clay vessels and industrial elements. Beachy surf-style objects true to Sylvia's lifestyle bring a little bit of fun to the unique space. Canopied outdoor areas are lofty and light, with textiles creating atmosphere while allowing the sunshine to filter in.

The cane house is my favorite spot, with the greens and blues I love inside and out. Its paned

windows, canvas slipcovers, birdcages and white-washed surfaces give it an airy feel. Rows of terra-cotta pots and lots of canvas and crumbling materials keep it from feeling too feminine.

The "Uphouse" guest cottage is simple, fresh and inviting. All the layers of textiles, comfy casual furnishings and bleached-out tones of biscuit, cream and white make it feel like a perfect summer getaway year round. The outside porch looks upon lawns filled with fragrant datura dangling with blossoms, making it all the more dreamy.

I photographed the breathtaking gardens for *House and Home* and had the pleasure of being a guest, listening to tropical rainstorms at night and waking to rainbows for my morning walk. In the mango grove, Zen touches with Indonesian artifacts add to an eclectic feel. I particularly love how all the succulents, orchids and tropical flora drape in abundance in gorgeous antique jardinières.

The cane house is my favorite spot, with the greens and blues I love inside and out. Its paned windows, canvas slipcovers, birdcages and white-washed surfaces give it an airy feel.

Owner Sylvia Hamilton Kerr and her interior designer sister, Nina Hamilton, transformed the ruins of a nineteenth-century sugar mill into an otherwordly paradise lush with botanicals and rich patina. Haiku Mill's breathtaking beauty makes it a dream wedding destination that's sure to captivate with its magical spell.

141

urban bohemian

Like a true gypsy, Kaili Zevenbergen keeps evolving and changing her home. Her personal look in both fashion and interiors is stylish and feminine, with a touch of bohemia. She's not afraid to invest her time in rental spaces, to personalize and transform them into her own paradise. Starting with the quality, character-filled bones of heritage buildings, she combines a touch of Zen, a touch of glamour and some understated earthy accents to create a spellbinding atmosphere.

First an avid customer, then part-time employee at my shop, Kaili would try things out on a regular basis. Treasures would go back and forth as she experimented and refined her look. The results are layered, lush, tactile, romantic. She has a great way of incorporating feathery materials like Moroccan rugs and blankets, and adding hits of shine and sparkle with natural crystals and metals. Using large, freestanding furnishings and draping textiles, she defines areas and creates intimacy within an otherwise open-concept space.

A savvy thrifter and collector, Kaili is great at repurposing and refurbishing furniture, seeing a new way of using something old. I've captured two of her city apartments, and while each is unique, they both have her similar touches woven throughout.

Kaili transformed this bathroom into a lush, exotic lair. Succulents, sea fans, tarnished silver and brass elements combine with the old clawfoot tub and exposed brick to create an impressive sanctuary. She cleverly cascades a vintage seashell plant hanger in front of the rough concrete wall, adding whimsy and softness.

I love how Kaili, in her previous apartment, chose driftwood and large seashells from our shop and made them feel at home amongst more glamorous accessories. You can see here (and on page 115) how she's been authentic in her style yet allowed her spaces to evolve and shift as she's refined her look.

savary island

Some of my happiest childhood memories were formed on this special island. Our family had a little cabin at Indian Point, steps away from the fine white sand dunes, beach grasses and shallow warm sea that would stretch out forever. We fished with our father and beachcombed for sand dollars and huge, white clamshells that dotted the shoreline. We'd feed eagles on the shore and explore tidal pools for sea anemones and starfish.

Years later, when I had the opportunity to revisit the island to photograph the funky prefab Pan-Abode cottages of the Tidey family, I was over the moon. I already knew April Tidey as a talented designer and friend who frequented my shop for unusual treasures, both for herself and for her clients. I had previously captured her unique sense of style in her city lofts. She is a master of the mix when it comes to quirky, hip, eclectic spaces. She has a more lively color palette than mine, and a knack for mixing midcentury furnishings together with a playful twist.

I knew April's Savary escape would be beachy, unpretentious and inviting, and indeed it was. The dreamy setting is made even more so by the deep meadow out front leading to a bluff that drops off into steep dunes to the ocean below. Canvas sailcloths are cleverly strung over the decks that look out upon the brilliant sea, creating a sense of both shelter and airiness.

This is a place where the door is always open to friends, family, neighbors and four-legged creatures. Originally trained as a landscape designer, April has done a great job of connecting two separate structures with a raised-deck patio, allowing for long summer days to be enjoyed both indoors and out. A plank dining table and cool old surveyor's tent allow for plenty of extra guests, while the funky outdoor shower truly makes one feel connected to the beachy outdoors. Open-paned windows with moon shells and pebbles on the sills, casually propped arbutus branches (indigenous to this area) and lacy bits of ocean finds bring nature in. Old, patinated mirrored surfaces, vintage bamboo furniture, bark cloth pillows and hurricane candles, all artfully placed, add to the relaxed beach shack feel.

Trained as a landscape designer, April Tidey has done a great job of connecting two Pan-Abode cottages with outdoor decking to allow for long summer days enjoyed both indoors and out. Cleverly strung sailcloths create atmospheric shelter.

Moon shells and pebbles on
windowsills, casually propped
arbutus branches indigenous
to the area, and lacy bits of
ocean finds bring nature in.

While each of these places is magical and unique in its own way, I am inspired by common themes that relate to my "natural eclectic" sensibilities. A tactile quality to the materials used in the homes, and a welcoming sense of comfort. A quirky mix of natural finds combined with treasures new and old. An authentic, personalized feeling and an integral connection to the local area and landscape.

All of these places also just happen to be less than an hour from the sea.

comfort,
connection
and
celebration

HOW WE INTERACT each day with our environment
and those we care about is what makes up a life.
Creating with love, sharing, caring, observing
with appreciation and gratitude—it's practices like these
that help us give a sense of meaning to our household. The
ephemeral things such as laughter and flowers blooming
on the windowsill are what really bring a place to life and
make a house a home. To experience the simple, soothing
moments that give us a sense of comfort, we need to slow
down and live with intention.

Conjure the feeling of glee while blowing out birthday
candles or returning home to find a loved one baking
cookies. Close your eyes and imagine stepping barefoot into
a garden. The smell of beeswax combined with smoke. The
kneading paws and soft lulling purr of a kitten. When we
tend to things we love with attention and care, we encourage them to flourish and grow. This can apply to ourselves,

Fresh rosemary, lavender and mint make perfect little bouquets and are lovely as fresh touches on a dinner plate. For this setting I could not resist my namesake flower.

friends, family, pets and even plants. Bring a blanket to a loved one, light a fire, offer a cup of tea. Run a long, hot, soothing bubble bath. Place flowers at a bedside table. Prepare a special meal to mark a meaningful occasion or, better yet, make every day feel more special.

When I host events, I combine fruits, florals, herbs and greenery into my food platters. I mix in vintage props, light candles and use unusual containers, like little old bottles in which I might place single stems. I always have to encourage guests to dig in, as they are so enchanted with the display they don't want to disrupt it! But enjoyment is what it is all about. When we nurture others through acts of beauty and thoughtfulness, we nurture ourselves.

I find cooking, baking, entertaining, gardening and quiet time with loved ones and pets so satisfying and grounding. Even during the holiday season, when running a shop can be very demanding, I always make time for baking from scratch. I love the hands-on aspect of it all, kneading the dough, rolling it out, forming the shapes—it reminds me of my days making pottery. I use old wooden rolling pins, ceramic mixing bowls and vintage baking ware and utensils. The whole process is so rewarding that it somehow makes me feel nurtured as well as nurturing.

Every year I make iced sugar cookies for my sister. As children we would make them together, decorated with gobs of garish bright icing and jujubes. My grownup versions are much more elegant, but the result is the same. The nostalgic memories bring my sister a feeling of love and excitement as she bites into the crunchy bells and stars. Seeing the joy on others' faces as they savor the fruits of my labor is what the season of giving is all about for me.

We can express nurturance even in the tending of a garden. I derive a great sense of joy from getting my hands in the earth and watching things grow. Gardening is a very meditative and grounding task that keeps me in the present. It reminds me of the delicate shifts in the seasons and the interconnected nature of all things. You can bring nature in by growing herbs on a windowsill, on the tiniest balcony garden or even on your kitchen counter. Use them for fresh flavors in your food but also as small arrangements. Sprigs of rosemary, lavender and fresh mint make perfect little bouquets and are also lovely as fresh touches on a dinner plate. I add dried organic rose petals to my morning black tea for a sweet, unusual depth of flavor, and I love to pick fresh lavender from my garden and add it into my cooking and baking. By placing a few fresh stems of lavender in a jar and filling it with sugar, you can impart a complex herbal taste to your sweetener. Vintage mason jars filled with lavender sugar make lovely hostess gifts.

Mark the turning of the seasons and create personalized ways of celebrating your own traditions. Use your imagination to turn everyday moments into special settings.

ECLECTIC GARDENS
Try bringing whimsical
eclectic touches such as
fishing floats, seashells
or even festive baubles
into your garden for
extra visual effect.

YOU CAN EXTEND the feeling of your home outdoors by bringing rustic antique treasures and eclectic touches out into your patio or garden. Decorative iron chairs make fabulous pedestals for planters. It doesn't matter if the iron is old and rusty and starts to fall apart over time—let it age and develop more patina. The undulating forms of branches look wonderful placed in large planters for vines to grow around, and gnarly pieces of driftwood from the beach can look beautiful artfully propped on a wooden deck.

In the fall and winter, when the garden can look a little bit weary, try adding large pinecones, seashells and ornamental gourds to help fill in the spaces. You can use moss, stones and seashells around the base of planters once perennials have gone dormant beneath the soil. Flower containers and jardinières, too, can have little additions beyond the living green elements. Fishing floats bring in extra visual interest to vessels and water features (as long as the raccoons don't take them). You can even bring festive baubles out into your garden. Tuck them within the planters and containers at your front entrance. Glass and metal baubles are perfect for this as they're impervious to moisture.

Most holidays mark historical and religious events that are associated with particular seasons. While keeping with the mood of the season, do try to use your imagination and go beyond using the same predictable colors and motifs year to year.

I created this vignette as a
lighter twist on autumn tones
for a fall harvest celebration.

At Christmastime I love to decorate in an icy wintry palette I describe as "an ethereal Noel." I collect vintage mercury glass ornaments in tones of silver, white, chartreuse, pale lavender, frosty blues and turquoise. I like simple spheres that remind me of sweetly colored birds' eggs, and I collect forms such as birds, pinecones and icicles as well—things that feel natural on a tree. Sometimes I forgo a tree altogether and just fill large glass vases with my baubles or hang the featherweight spheres on fine white branches. They're so fragile and speak so much about nostalgia and special moments of the past. I often tuck just one into a little nest and leave it on display all the way from the turning of the New Year to Easter.

I encourage you to create personalized ways of acknowledging and celebrating your own customs and traditions and marking the turn of the seasons. Try making simple celebrations out of everyday moments as well, with simple acts like lighting candles or using linen napkins. Take time to unwind and reconnect with your creative self. Make things by hand, use nature for decoration, and start your own traditions. Year round, I wrap gifts with kraft paper, recycled tissue, twine and old silk ribbons, and I might just add a tiny branch or leaf to the package.

ETHEREAL NOEL

I love to decorate in a wintry palette. Vintage mercury glass ornaments come in forms such as icicles, pinecones and birds—things that feel natural on a tree.

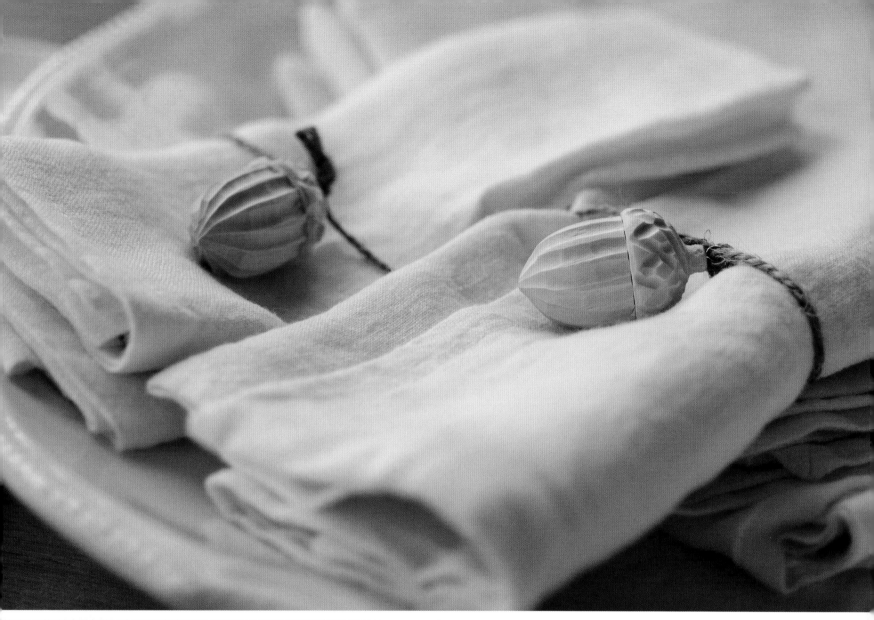

Growing and makings things can bring a lasting sense of satisfaction for you and your loved ones—a sense that endures far beyond the experience of shopping or ordering online. Make meaningful choices in your life and home that give you and others a feeling of peace, comfort and love.

the serendipitous collector

WHEN I WAS a young teen, I went berry picking with my mom at one of those U-pick farms where you save money by picking your own raspberries and strawberries. I happened to notice an old bentwood chair in the field. It was faded and some of the wood was split, but it still retained such charm. I asked the farmer whether I could buy it. He looked at me with amusement and set a price of two dollars. Agreed. My first find! And my first experience as a "picker," quite literally. My mom was a little confounded, but once I got the chair home and cleaned it up, she could see that, indeed, I had found a treasure.

Picking has now become very popular, with TV shows making junking, thrifting and flea-market scouring more mainstream. The notion of embracing all things nostalgic is wonderful. I encourage you to have fun doing your own picking—seek out fabulous authentic pieces that speak to you.

With an adventurous spirit, seek out seasonal fairs such as this one held by Déjà Vu Vintage Market, to find treasures that speak to you.

Formulaic thinking that has you believing that decor can only be found in the big furniture stores limits your choices. If you can't get out to a flea market, try supporting your local thrift stores, antique shops and eclectic boutiques—these are all great sources for original finds. At my shop, I always say we don't do "new to look old." Why choose a poorly made, mass-produced repro version that often has less charm and a higher price tag than the original? Convenience perhaps, but the cost is not just out of your wallet; it's also to the environment. When buying new, I say go for well-functioning clean-lined contemporary pieces and integrate them with true old finds. It's the mix that keeps things interesting. With a little resourcefulness and an adventurous spirit, you can find things that have been lovingly used and have a natural, hand-hewn patina.

WHILE I ADORE the charm of vintage and antique items, I'm always mindful to avoid the "granny factor" or items that just feel too kitsch. A little bit of whimsy can be lovely, but do consider the enduring allure of timeless objects. When considering a purchase, ask yourself, is it beautiful to behold? Does it bring me joy? Does it have personal meaning or sentimental value? Does it connect me to memories, experiences and travels? Is it well crafted, and will it stand the test of time in both quality and style? If not, pass it up.

Okay, so let's get treasure hunting! Traveling for antiques and bespoke finds at flea markets around the world is truly one of my favorite pastimes. You really get a sense of a country, its culture and its customs when you immerse yourself in a local market. Depending on where you travel, the market might be called a swap

meet, car boot sale, antique fair, rummage sale or *brocante*. No matter the term, they all give me a thrill!

You never really know what special find will call to you once you get to a market. This is part of the fun. You might find quaint chandeliers, old botanical prints, rustic pottery, antique books, stacks of linens. For those who collect something in particular, it can be like searching for a needle in a haystack. I'm a little more organic in my buying trips for the shop, allowing serendipity to unfold. Yet, while I never plan what I am going to unearth on my travels, somehow a concise continuity reveals itself so that, in the end, I have a fabulous grouping of objects that work together. I'm always so excited to bring back the finds I've chosen and carefully incorporate them into my shop displays.

Much like people, markets each have their own personality. Some can be quite formal and traditional, others more casual and haphazard, others enchanting and beautifully staged (yet with goods so pricey they are unattainable). That said, I've picked up the most exquisite collectibles in the most humble of junky little markets and walked away with an incredible bargain from the most opulent of fairs.

Rummaging in search of a great find can be rather arduous, but it's so rewarding. By day's end, your arms are full, your hands are dirty, your pockets empty. Your mind is spinning from converting words and currencies and bartering. You can't imagine how you'll fit it all into your luggage, let alone make it back to your hotel. But it is intoxicating.

I've scoured markets in England, Holland, Belgium, Croatia and France, as well as ones I've stumbled upon locally while on road trips at home. When visiting my sister in Italy, we'd head off to picturesque towns like Luca or to the larger historic city Arezzo, which is known internationally for its large fair the first Sunday of the month.

In the United States, I attended the sprawling Brimfield market in Massachusetts. This market is so massive it was overwhelming even for a pro like me, with fields and fields brimming with country antiques.

Of all the countries I've visited, I find France to have the most captivating markets with the most beautiful selection of goods. During my two years in Paris and on my many visits and buying trips over the years, I've come to learn which ones are the best to attend on certain days, what sections to bypass, which markets have the best deals—and at which ones the early bird really does get the worm.

LA FAUVETTE À TÈTE NOIRE

Edouard Travies del.

I'll never forget this captivating display I stumbled upon at the fountain of historic Saint-Sulpice church. The enormous old clamshells draped with brilliant peonies, apricots and cherries were so striking juxtaposed against all the other treasures. The French really have a flair for displays!

I've never been a morning person, yet remarkably, on market days suddenly my sleepy self is up and out the door, imagining all the most alluring finds rapidly disappearing as I impatiently make my way along crowded little streets to the hustle and bustle of barkers and dealers. (The only other exception is when a tropical setting with a coral sunrise and the sound of waves beckons me to wake and put my toes in the sand.)

My two favorite regular weekend markets in Paris are the *marché aux puces* (flea markets) at Saint-Ouen and Porte de Vanves. Of the two, the market at Vanves is a smaller, more manageable choice for those who just want to have a pleasurable morning doing a little antiquing as

part of their Paris adventures. Throughout the year, weeklong open-air brocantes are held along different streets in Paris. You can spot them by the colored awnings and the gathering of curious crowds. At least once a year, a beautifully appointed open-air antique show is held in the square of Place Saint-Sulpice, with its charming surrounding shops and cafés.

For me, exploring the countryside of France, going from village to village visiting smaller brocantes, each on its own day of the week, is the most satisfying of all. It can be quite arduous on hot summer days, so remember to pack a big tote bag, comfy walking shoes and bottled water. Take advantage of nearby patisseries and boulangeries, and allow yourself an occasional break (and treat) so you're not exhausted by day's end.

One of the most abundant places for those who love design, decor and antiques is L'isle-sur-la-Sorgue, in the south of France near Avignon. Termed the Venice of France for the river that wends around it, this town swells twice a year with buyers from around the world gathering for its big fair. Yet every day in this town is a picker's dream. The streets are lined with home decor boutiques, historic cafés and lovely courtyards just sprawling with furnishings and bric-à-brac. An old converted train station warehouses a plethora of antiques to delight all tastes. Not to be overlooked are the colorful open-air stands of fresh fruit and flowers and savory Provençal delights at every turn—truly a feast for all senses.

The small neighboring towns in this Vaucluse region each have their own breathtaking scenery and unique flavor. Gordes is built all of stone. Roussillon is built against a dramatic backdrop of ochre mines, the whole town appearing as if it's been painted with a brushstroke of terra-cotta. Villeneuve-lès-Avignon is a quaint village just minutes from Avignon. With lovely little hotels, smaller crowds and an enticing Saturday market, it is a great town to stay in for a night or two. Farther along the French Riviera, Nice has a lovely brocante held on Mondays in the flower market at Cours Saleya. I adore the open feeling of this place, with the softly faded facades of the historic buildings lining the courtyard and the Côte d'Azur sea just minutes away.

The charming streets of L'isle-sur-la-Sorgue in the south of France are sprawling with antiques and bric-à-brac, home decor boutiques and historic cafés.

Nice has a lovely brocante market held on Mondays in the flower market at Cours Saleya. I adore the open feeling of this place with the softly faded facades and the Côte d'Azur sea just minutes away.

While I'm not a morning person, on market days I'm up and out the door in pursuit of alluring finds.

Piles of linens folded and stacked in an armoire make my heart beat faster. In the markets of Europe, you can find exceptional cloth creations. Having worked as a textile designer, I just love to go through fabrics looking for antique textiles, rustic laces and trims. I have a special affinity for them. Not only do they take me back to my roots, I also cherish them for the painstaking labor of love that goes into every single little hand stitch in an eyelet lace. I find it unfathomable to imagine the detail and care that went into everyday linens, let alone into the creation of the fine draperies and tapestries that adorned castle walls and churches for centuries.

Delicate and fragile when exposed to the elements, fabrics can break down over the years. Some fibers, like silk, are more fragile than others. Linen and flax are perhaps the sturdiest fabrics, even stronger wet than dry, which is why you can pick up old linen sheets that have survived centuries of use. I admire the longevity of these functional items made with love to serve a family. Held with loving hands, providing warmth and comfort, they still endure, after years and years of use, many for the most utilitarian purposes, such as gathering grains.

In fact, grain sack fabric has become all the rage in interiors. Their thick weaves and hand-hewn rusticity make grain sacks ideal for upholstery, big, sturdy pillows and table runners. It's hard to imagine the labor that went into spinning, weaving and sewing these bags when, today, we just grab a plastic bag out of the cupboard and throw it away the next day.

Sacks are often embroidered with monograms, and I was so delighted to find this one with an NE—for Natural Eclectic!

P^on 440
METRES FIXES
N° 12
Rayonne

When antiquing, let
yourself be inspired
by the locations and
experiences as well.
The Vaucluse region
of France is a treasure
in itself. Built against a
dramatic backdrop of
ochre cliffs, the facades
in the town of Rousillon
seem to have been
painted with a brush
stroke of terra-cotta.

WHETHER YOU FIND a treasure in an antique fair or discarded in a back alley, salvaging and repurposing is fabulous for the environment as well as being very satisfying and creative. Bringing new life to things is the essence of recycling. It's great to see a diamond in the rough and find the value in old materials.

From sun-bleached boards drifting up on the beach to industrial hardware culled from an old factory, things can be transformed cleverly from one function to another. As a bonus, most old materials have authentic battered and worn surfaces that could never be manufactured or

reproduced with such depth and charm. So, while you may not be collecting treasures for the sake of the environment, indirectly you are making lifestyle choices that benefit our planet.

They say it's not the destination, it's the journey. I would say this is true of treasure hunting, collecting, salvaging. It's not just about what you end up with. The experience itself is such an adventure. The allure of the old treasures you find becomes interwoven with your treasured memories of their discovery, adding your own history to the layers of patina surrounding the item you cherish.

9

the
natural
forager

A FTER A DAY of antiquing in the countryside, I love to get out for a walk. I just adore rustic rural landscapes, and I dream of one day having a farm. I'll pet horses at a field's edge, take pictures of old barns and pick branches and dried grasses along the winding roads. If I'm lucky to find fallen fruit in an abandoned old orchard, I'll grab an armful and take the lovely speckled forms home to place into a bowl for display. Treasure hunting and foraging out in pastoral settings or along seashores is as much a beloved pastime for me as antiquing at fairs.

For those of us who respect and appreciate the beauty of nature, there is paradox in wanting to bring natural found objects into our homes. If we're not prudent in how we harvest natural finds, we can hurt the very thing we love, the natural environment! I am more mindful now of every little thing I take from the earth, careful where I step and what I take. I might pluck a curling piece of birch bark from a decaying log or pick a few seashells from the beach to place at home amongst other treasures, but I'm mindful not to disturb a natural ecosystem.

The land naturally creates a mulching system for the seasons, a time of protection, a time for exposure, a time of blooming and abundance, a time to go quiet into the earth. Mother Nature can be our best teacher if we just observe how she naturally protects herself. The natural world demonstrates beautifully that everything works in concert, going out of balance only when we interfere. It is our responsibility to be informed and proactively involved in the wellness of our earth.

Gather and forage with restraint. If you want to pick moss, stumps and lichen, try to do so in areas already being actively forested or slated for development as opposed to an untouched forest. The cycle of life is something to behold—a fine balance. Life springs anew from dormant ground. Seeds and bulbs turn to sprigs of life that become fully branched trees. These trees then produce seeds and cones that fall to the earth, enriching the soil, feeding the insects, the birds, ourselves.

Left to dry in situ, many weeds will retain their seeds with flowery tops preserved in starry or fanning shapes.

At home in my garden, I plant beautiful blooms, yet I often find the weeds that come up to be just as charming. Scavenging for roadside weeds is a great way to harvest naturally occurring rampant overgrowth. Some plants overtake and smother others, so their removal can actually be beneficial to our planet. Queen Anne's lace, with its bright green feathery foliage, tall stems and lacy white tops, is one such invasive species. It grows so abundantly you can take massive armfuls and use it to make large, loose, full arrangements. Left to dry naturally in situ, many reeds and weeds will retain their seeds with flowering tops preserved in starry or fanning shapes. Their light yet sturdy stalks make them easy to gather and arrange in large vessels. Hydrangea blossoms trimmed in late summer will last for quite some time in water, with the petals beautifully burnishing into a deeper autumn tinge over time.

One year something self-seeded in one of my planters. I was tempted to remove it, yet curious what it might become. Over a span of a few years, this spindly sprout grew taller and taller, until it became a finely branched little tree. One spring it suddenly presented delicate pink petals—cherry blossoms!

This lesson about letting things be applies to insects, too. I never use pesticides. I do not want to harm any living creatures. We are naive to think we can save the cute and helpful insects, such as honeybees and ladybugs, while destroying the "inconvenient" pests. Pesticides trickle down into the soil and our water systems and affect us all, including the beneficial insects and the birds and creatures that feed on them.

Each year the ponderosa pines above my patio drop their cones onto the deck. I gather them like a little squirrel and use them in my festive displays at the shop. One day this past spring, I was

Fallen magnolia leaves turn into gauzy skeletal forms. If you're standing under one of these magnificent trees, look not just up but down.

out on my terrace shooting a still life of branches for this chapter when I heard a *wzzzzz wzzzzz.* Looking up, I spotted a brilliant flitting jewel of a creature hovering above me. And then I saw the tiny fluffy nest in the juncture of a long, dangling branch—hummingbirds nesting in the pines! Immediately, I contacted the tree arborist who was scheduled for a visit to make sure this little family would be safe. Observing these remarkable creatures as they feed in my garden each day has brought me so much joy.

If you see someone out pruning trees, take this chance to pick up some branches for free. It's remarkable how discarded branches that seem lifeless will come back if you bring them in and put them in water. In this way, you can "force" ornamental dogwood, forsythia and cherry blossom branches to bloom early. Reviving mystery branches is especially delightful, as you wait to see what beautiful surprise flower might unfold!

Among my all-time-favorite flowering trees are magnolias. Before their fuzzy buds open, they look like pussy willows. Their blossoms can vary from softly unfurling starry shapes to voluptuous waxy forms with massive upturned petals. Magnolias line Vancouver streets near my home, and in late winter I keep my eye out for stray branches that might have fallen in a storm or been nipped off by a truck. Fallen magnolia leaves retain their gauzy skeletal forms forever, so next time you're standing under one of these gorgeous trees, look not just up but down.

A still life of treasures, with curvilinear branches and fan coral, and a large, crocheted-cotton overhead lampshade add organic interest to my dining nook, which often does double duty as an office.

190 ■

I placed magnolia branches I found at curbside into a large, old teapot that has a handle and spout with a *faux bois* ("fake wood") design. With its lid broken, the pot itself makes the most wonderful vase. (This is another example of using your imagination and seeing things in a different way, instead of discarding what seems broken.) Within one day, these branches started to bud. Each morning when I rose, I was captivated by how much they had changed overnight. I could not have anticipated just how gloriously they would bloom and unfold, reaching out alongside my beloved tri-fold mirror. I would catch reflections of them from all angles as I made my morning tea. Their delicate yet heady scent filled the room. On day four, the flowers became papery and the edges turned brown, like tea-stained cloth. Petals started to drop. Yet little bursts of green were peeking out as new leaves burst to life.

While I don't love the look of technology, this is the reality of living in our current times, so I just do my best to embrace it! My computer sits on an old pine table with fabulously worn layers of paint. I find that by juxtaposing sleek electronics with rustic surfaces and natural found objects, we can have the best of old worlds—a little bit of modern offset by organic forms.

WHILE FORAGING along country roads and forest floors brings me delight, I just adore beachcombing! A day by the seaside, swimming, searching for beach glass or perfect pebbles, is a simple activity everyone can enjoy. I find it meditative to search along the coast for eye-catching stones, bits of old china that have washed up, pearly shells and ornamental pieces of driftwood. I especially like oval pebbles that emulate an egg form, simple stones with stripes, and flat, smooth grey, green or black ones. I place them in a wooden bowl or along a windowsill, or I stack them to create little towers or pedestals for other finds—humble touchstones and mementos from my travels and day trips.

As a merchant, artist and consumer, I have become increasingly aware of my own footprint on the environment and its impact on living creatures great and small. While I delight in searching for seashells bleached at the shore's edge, I would never take them from the ocean alive and dry them out just for "decorative" purposes. Sand dollars, starfish and sea urchins are living creatures that inhabit shallow waters and tidal pools. The skeletal forms they leave behind have magical shapes and intricate patterns. Just make sure they're not alive before you scoop them up and take them home. A few for a windowsill perhaps, but don't get greedy. Even in their afterlife, these shells contribute to

As a merchant and consumer, I've become increasingly aware of my footprint. The craggy silhouettes of coral are so lovely mixed with beachy finds and antiques, yet to preserve their fragile ecosystem, I've made a decision to choose only from antique or vintage collections harvested years ago.

the delicate ecosystem. Be it tiny grains of sand or minuscule ferns, all provide a foundation and shelter for other forms of life.

Many of our ocean reefs are now protected, and rightly so. You can still legally purchase some species of coral and shells from tropical import companies, but please be sure they're ethically sourced. I find the craggy, curvilinear silhouettes of coral so exceptionally lovely to incorporate into a display with beachy finds and antiques. The variety of their forms is fascinating. Yet, to preserve them, I have made a decision to choose only from antique or vintage collections harvested years ago.

Similarly, I find antlers to be such a beautiful shape and symbol, their lyrically branched forms bringing an elegant line to a display. Many people don't realize that deer shed their antlers each year. I prefer to collect the whole antler in its original state as it has naturally molted.

Imagining it dropping to a mossy floor as a majestic buck roams the forest makes all the difference to me. Mine is a small effort and far from perfect, but with conscientious small gestures, we can each do our part to help the planet and all of us who share it.

WHETHER YOU LIVE in a city, a town or out in the countryside, I encourage you to forage within your environs and to embrace all the seasons. It is natural for me to feel like cocooning on days that seem dark or drizzly. And yet, once I venture out beyond the shelter of my home, into the complex smell of trees and damp earth, and experience the surprising amount of light emanating from the sky even on a grey day, I become invigorated. I'm in the moment. Summer rain can smell so sweet as it falls upon a warm sidewalk or a field of dry golden grasses. All of nature is refreshed. Stormy weather really isn't quite so bad when you're enveloped in it walking in the woods, cozy with the one you love, or standing on a shore feeling a misty cascade as the sky melts into the sea.

So I will end on this note. Get out into the elements and explore. Seek and create beauty in your life. Be mindful of nature's precious balance so that we may continue to live connected to its glorious abundance for years to come. Define what a sense of place means to you. Tap into your creative self, and find your own expressive voice. Cherish the wonder of nature. Nurture it and those you love.

{ ACKNOWLEDGMENTS }

M Y LIFE HAS been touched by so many. I am grateful for all the abundance that has come into my life, and for the wisdom and support others have shared along the way.

I'd like to thank my mother for the gift of language.

My father for showing me the gifts of the sea.

My sister for her unwavering love and belief in me.

Craig Anderl, for having been my dear companion on so many of these journeys.

I could not have asked for a better team than Figure 1 Publishing—they believed in my vision, guiding me every step of the way to help make my dream of a book come to fruition. Thanks to Jessica Sullivan for her beautiful eye for design and sensitivity to my wishes in the daunting task of bringing all my words and imagery to life on these pages. A heartfelt thanks to Marial Shea, my kind editor, who nurtured the story out of me with such care and respect.

I am so grateful to Suzanne Dimma for her touching foreword and enthusiastic support of my project. Gratitude to the generosity of Mr. Yosef Wosk, who saw the potential in my book long before it unfolded. My sincere appreciation to those who allowed me to capture and share their special places within these pages. To Rick and Lara Irwin, thank you for providing the sanctuary of your cottage.

To all my friends and family who have been there for me, especially in the cathartic year that was devoted to making this book—thank you. Your laughter, comfort and friendship helped anchor me in my purpose during this powerful time of creative expression.

Eternal gratitude to Brent Boechler for helping me see I belonged to the beauty of the world. While you're no longer of this earth, your own beautiful imprint lives on forever.

None of this would have been possible without the loyal following of my wonderful clients who have crossed my paths over the years, offering generous support and such warm words of appreciation and encouragement. You have been like another family to me.

{ CREDITS }

FRONT AND BACK COVERS
Photographed and styled by Heather Ross

ALL PHOTOGRAPHY BY HEATHER ROSS
with the exception of pages 165 right and
184 by Craig Anderl, and page 176 by
Debbie Custock

**STYLING AND VIGNETTES
BY HEATHER ROSS**

Pages iii, viii, 1, 8 to 11, 36, 44, 67, 70,
84 to 88, 90 to 92, 101, 106, 114, 130, 156,
158 to 160, 161 to 164, 184 to 193

At Heather Ross Natural Eclectic
boutique, Vancouver, BC: Pages vi, 4 to 7,
21, 24, 28, 32, 37, 48, 75, 78–79, 81 to 83,
107 to 113, 116, 119, 166, 167, 186, 190

**ORIGINAL ARTWORK
BY HEATHER ROSS**

Pages 3, 21, 32, 36, 37, 55, 79, 104, 116,
164, 166, 205, back cover

ON LOCATION DESIGN CREDITS
WEST VANCOUVER, BC
Architecture and interior design by
Zacharko Yustin Architects
Pages 12 to 15

HAIKU MILL, MAUI
Sylvia Hamilton Kerr
Nina Hamilton – Napanee Design
Pages 17 top, 19 bottom right, 118, 136 to 141

EBB TIDE, ROBERTS CREEK, BC
Interiors by Lara Irwin
Pages 22, 30 right, 41, 49 left, 84 to 86, 90, 91,
117, 120–121, 124 to 129, 157 top, 160, 161

VANCOUVER, BC
Interior styling by Kaili Zevenbergen
Pages 31 middle, 115, 142 to 147

WHISTLER, BC
Sophie Burke Design
Pages 45, 56, 195

ITALIAN FARMHOUSE, JESI, ITALY
Interiors by Janet Ross
Pages 130 to 135

SAVARY ISLAND, BC
April Tidey Design
Pages 148 to 153

HEATHER ROSS is known for her natural aesthetic, inspired both by her West Coast upbringing and her time spent living and antiquing in Paris. Her artfully curated boutique has earned a loyal following since opening in Vancouver in 2001. A creative force of nature with a background in painting, printmaking, ceramics and textile design, Heather is also recognized for her work as a writer, stylist and photographer in many top lifestyle magazines, and her evocative artworks have been placed in numerous feature films and international collections. When not involved in her many creative projects, she enjoys cooking, gardening, beachcombing and treasure hunting. A true animal lover, she cares deeply about all creatures great and small. This is her first book.

Photography by Heather Ross
Design by Jessica Sullivan
Editing by Marial Shea
Copy editing by Grace Yaginuma

Printed and bound in China by
1010 Printing International, Ltd.
Distributed in the U.S. by Publishers
Group West

Figure 1 Publishing Inc.
Vancouver BC Canada
www.figure1pub.com